MW00604698

FLOURISH

—

SESSIONS 1 - 6

our prayer

That He may grant you to be strengthened with power through his Spirit in your inner being, [17] so that Christ may dwell in your hearts through faith—that you, being rooted and grounded in love, [18] may have strength to comprehend with all the saints what is the breadth and length and height and depth, [19] and to know the love of Christ that surpasses knowledge, that you may be filled with all the fullness of God. [20] Now to Him who is able to do far more abundantly than all that we ask or think, according to the power at work within us, [21] to Him be glory in the church and in Christ Jesus throughout all generations, forever and ever. Amen.

EPHESIANS 3:16-20 ESV

TABLE
OF
CONTENTS

—

SESSIONS 1 - 6

+ MENTOR GUIDELINES

TABLE OF CONTENTS

(continued)

▶ MENTOR GUIDELINES / p.280

THIS IS THE BEGINNING OF SOMETHING

beautiful

—

Welcome to Year Two of FLOURISH mentoring! We pray that this brand new year will be an opportunity to build on the solid foundation of faith in Jesus that began in what Christ did in your heart through Year One of FLOURISH. We are praying this will be a year of growth as God continues to draw you into His Word to discover a richer understanding of His heart and perfect love as He invites you to come face to face with the truth, with yourself and with His unending and transforming love. So, it is with much joy that we open this second year of FLOURISH with this goal: to position ourselves at the feet of Jesus, and join together to become women who are rooted so deeply in His Word that we root in His unfailing Word, and bear fruit that comes from soaking in His promises and living by the fruit that comes from faithfully depending on Him.

We want you to start by believing that Jesus can break through both the thickest wall and the smallest barrier that attempts to hold you back from flourishing in the life He made you to live. As we begin, let us each surrender and with open arms embrace the journey ahead. Based on that sure footing, allow the Lord access to your full being, inviting Him to change in you whatever needs to be changed. As we begin to dive into the study and understanding of His words of life, we embrace the truth of Hebrews 12:1-2 as the desire of our heart. Hebrews reminds us to "Therefore, since we are surrounded by such a great cloud of witnesses, let us throw off everything that hinders and the sin that so easily entangles. And let us run with perseverance the race marked out for us, fixing our eyes on Jesus, the pioneer and perfecter of faith." Let's go! FLOURISH calls women to a higher standard of living. One where we wholeheartedly love & follow Jesus and aim to view our lives and circumstances through the lens of Scripture.

SESSION STEPS

01   Commit to meet with Jesus five times per week for the next twelve months. You determine when, where, and for how long.

02   Focus on the passages of Scripture and the daily assignment. Follow the readings for each day. Always end your time with God in prayer.

03   Meet with your mentor at the times you have agreed upon.

we love you!

THE GROVE / FLOURISH Team

FEMININE HEART

SESSION ONE

How can we even begin to comprehend this great love story that God has set into motion and accomplished for us, His crowning creation? Of course, the only place to begin is THE BEGINNING. The book of Genesis gives us a basic account understanding of God's original design for the world, for humanity, and even specifically for us as women.

Too often, believers have a haphazard relationship with the Scripture. Instead of reading within context, we jump around the Word with little understanding of the overall story or God's great heart for humanity. Because we haven't anchored ourselves properly in the Word, we may find ourselves weakened when we're faced with obstacles, overcome when confronted by temptation, and shrinking away when challenged by opposition. It's only when we know this awesome God who formed all things out of nothing (Gen. 1:1), who separated light from darkness (Gen 2:5), and declared His handiwork – you and I – to be "very good" (Gen 1:31), that we can ever hope to begin to understand who we were made to be.

This year we will center our time on God's Word with the goal of building solid study habits that give us a confidence to know – not a list of rules – but intimately know and trust our Savior Jesus Christ. As His words become written indelibly on our minds and hearts, we will more accurately see the unfolding story Jesus is writing – a story for His glory and for our good.

SESSION GOALS

THE FEMININE HEART

GOALS

- To help us see that we are designed by God for a unique and crucial purpose.
- To encourage us to prioritize a relationship with God before concentrating on other relational roles.
- To understand and embrace our current season of life (single, wife, mother) as an opportunity to know God and serve Him more fully.
- To learn dependency on the Holy Spirit to enable us to thrive in our role as a single woman, wife and/or mother.

QUESTIONS

- How does understanding Eve help you understand yourself?
- What new discovery did you make about your role as a woman and how does that change the way you see yourself and interact with others?
- What's most challenging aspect of the season of life you are in right now?
- How can you know Jesus better through these challenges?

FEMININE HEART

MADE IN THE IMAGE OF GOD

—

GENESIS 1:24-27

[24] And God said, "Let the land produce living creatures according to their kinds: the livestock, the creatures that move along the ground, and the wild animals, each according to its kind." And it was so. [25] God made the wild animals according to their kinds, the livestock according to their kinds, and all the creatures that move along the ground according to their kinds. And God saw that it was good. [26] Then God said, "Let us make mankind in our image, in our likeness, so that they may rule over the fish in the sea and the birds in the sky, over the livestock and all the wild animals, and over all the creatures that move along the ground." [27] So God created mankind in his own image, in the image of God he created them; male and female he created them.

CREATED IN HIS IMAGE

In Scripture, God is revealed as Triune ("Tri" meaning 3, "Une" or "Unity" meaning one = Tri-unity or Trinity). That is, God has one essence but is revealed in three persons, the Father, the Son, and the Holy Spirit. The Godhead lives… past, present and future… in perfect fellowship together. Apart from basic theology, this is important to understand since it is part of His nature to exist in unbroken fellowship with other members of the Godhead. While volumes have been written about what it means for us to be "created in the image of God," the most basic understanding of it is that we, as human beings, resemble our Creator. And one of the unique ways we reflect Him is that we are made for fellowship, and, chiefly, fellowship with Him. While we can achieve and succeed at many things, until we make a relationship with Him our supreme priority, all other interests will leave us empty and unfulfilled. This week we will focus in on the one thing that supersedes all others… to know and be known by God.

SESSION QUESTIONS

—

WEEK ONE

DAY 01 Who am I? What is my purpose? What was I meant to do? These questions only find satisfying answers when we embrace our first and most basic calling: to love and be loved by God. Begin your study of this topic by reading through Psalm 63. What stands out to you as significant in these verses?

DAY 02 Make a list of things you are passionate about (ex. family, friends, bargain hunting, healthy eating, exercise, sports teams, etc.) Reread Psalm 63, noticing the passionate heart behind David's desire for God. How does this challenge you to reorder priorities and interests?

DAY 03 Compare verses 1 and 5 of Psalm 63. Write in your journal how you think David could be completely satisfied, yet at the same time be desperate for more of God. Include how you could encourage a similar state of contented longing.

DAY 04 Turn to 2 Samuel 15-16 to understand the likely situation in which David penned Psalm 63. How does what you read give new depth to his desire for the Lord? In your difficulties, which do you long for more: to be relieved from pain or to know God more? (Cross reference Phil. 3:10-14)

DAY 05 Underline the promise God gives to those who seek the Lord recorded in Jeremiah 29:11-14. Memorize these verses.

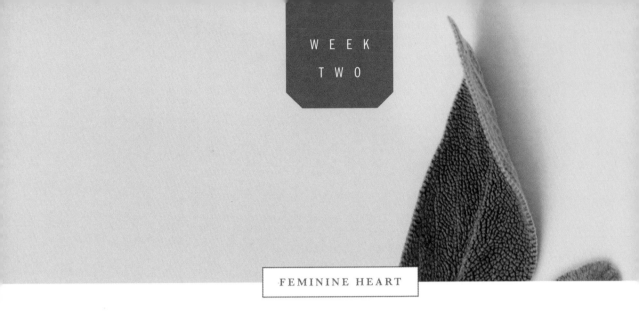

FEMININE HEART

BE FRUITFUL

—

GENESIS 1:24-28

24 And God said, "Let the land produce living creatures according to their kinds: the livestock, the creatures that move along the ground, and the wild animals, each according to its kind." And it was so. 25 God made the wild animals according to their kinds, the livestock according to their kinds, and all the creatures that move along the ground according to their kinds. And God saw that it was good. 26 Then God said, "Let us make mankind in our image, in our likeness, so that they may rule over the fish in the sea and the birds in the sky, over the livestock and all the wild animals, and over all the creatures that move along the ground."
27 So God created mankind in his own image, in the image of God he created them; male and female he created them. 28 God blessed them and said to them, "Be fruitful and increase in number…"

REACHING WELL BEYOND

Taken literally, Genesis 1:28 can evoke a variety of emotions. Joy and satisfaction flood the hearts of those who have loving and happy children. Painful memories surface for those who are estranged from their children or whose children have left the earth far too early. And bitter heartache may echo in the souls of those who desire to have families of their own, yet dwell in a place of unfulfilled longing. While raising offspring is a blessing of God to be celebrated and a responsibility to be carefully attended, the command to "be fruitful and multiply" isn't limited only to those with physical children. This week we will broaden our grasp of this command and widen our application to find it reaching well beyond the confines of only homes and families.

SESSION QUESTIONS

———

WEEK TWO

DAY 01 Read the entire passage on page 20 and then contemplate verse 28. Consider the meaning of the word "fruitful." On your own or with the help of a dictionary/thesaurus, make a list of synonyms. Pick the one you think that most accurately reflects the meaning it has for Christian women today.

DAY 02 Did you write the word "produce" in your list yesterday? In what ways do you "produce" by creating something of value and worth in your home, business, relationships, etc?

DAY 03 Turn to 1 Thessalonians 1:2-3. For what three things does Paul commend these believers? Notice also the manner in which each is accomplished as well. How could these be instrumental in becoming more fruitful?

DAY 04 Look up John 12:23-26. What does Jesus say is necessary to become truly fruitful? Write down how this might be relevant to areas of your life that are of great frustration. Include any experiences in which you can personally attest to the truth of Christ's words.

DAY 05 Read Psalm 144. Direct your attention to verse 5-8. In poetic language, David requests God to show Himself in his situation. In the most difficult situation that you face now, the one that continues to feel "unfruitful" and "barren," begin to make note of the ways (even in small things) that God "smokes" the mountains and sends forth "lightning". Keep an ongoing journal of how you see Him "show up" for you even in the middle of frustration and disappointment.

FEMININE HEART

SUBDUE & RULE

—

GENESIS 1:28-31

[28] God blessed them and said to them, "Be fruitful and increase in number; fill the earth and subdue it. Rule over the fish in the sea and the birds in the sky and over every living creature that moves on the ground." [29] Then God said, "I give you every seed-bearing plant on the face of the whole earth and every tree that has fruit with seed in it. They will be yours for food. [30] And to all the beasts of the earth and all the birds in the sky and all the creatures that move along the ground—everything that has the breath of life in it—I give every green plant for food." And it was so. [31] God saw all that he had made, and it was very good. And there was evening, and there was morning—the sixth day.

SUBDUE & RULE

Have you ever worked for a boss who just doesn't seem to have a clue what's going on? Maybe the managers are so focused on "managing" that they can't relate to the real needs of the customers and employees. If you've ever been there, you know that it's only a matter of time until the effectiveness of the whole business suffers and morale breaks down. A truly wise leader will be one who knows and cares about the people over whom he or she has authority. Without that knowledge the boss will quickly become distracted and ineffective. God delegated to Adam and Eve – and to us – authority to rule, but with that authority comes responsibility. This week we will explore the example of our perfect Ruler and come to understand better the specific areas that all believers are at all times commanded to rule and subdue.

SESSION QUESTIONS

———

WEEK THREE

01   Reflect on the passage for today, keying in on the last part of verse 28. Make notes about what you think it means for people to "subdue" and "rule" the earth. Look this verse up in several different translations to give added understanding. Write a list of the truths that stick out to you.

02   Read David's words recorded in 1 Chronicles 29:10-13, Psalm 86:8-18, and Psalm 145:13-16 to get more insight into God as supreme Ruler over the earth. With Him as our pattern, what do you conclude about how people are to rule? What does that teach you about your role in the story?

03   Biblical teacher Barbara Mouser* gives a clear definition of the word subdue: to bring under control by conquest and keep under control by diligent maintenance. Notice what Romans 7:7-25 says about the struggle all believers face. Pay special attention to verse 25 to identify through whom victory is achieved. Add any thoughts about what you learn to your journal.

04   God delegates areas of authority to us in which we need to exercise "control" and "maintenance" (home, work, relationships, self, etc). Read James 3, and write notes about what it says needs our constant vigilance to subdue. Include why you think James writes such strong words.

05   Continue reading James 4, noting the most effective way to subdue and "tame the tongue." Conclude your study by meditating on Psalm 19:14. Make this passage your daily prayer for the rest of this session.

*Mouser, Barbara K. "Mistress of the Domain." Five Aspects of Woman: A Biblical Theology of Femininity, WinePress Pub, 1995, p. 24.

FEMININE HEART

FREE FROM SHAME

—

GENESIS 2:19-25

[19] Now the Lord God had formed out of the ground all the wild animals and all the birds in the sky. He brought them to the man to see what he would name them; and whatever the man called each living creature, that was its name. [20] So the man gave names to all the livestock, the birds in the sky and all the wild animals. But for Adam no suitable helper was found. [21] So the Lord God caused the man to fall into a deep sleep; and while he was sleeping, he took one of the man's ribs and then closed up the place with flesh. [22] Then the Lord God made a woman from the rib he had taken out of the man, and he brought her to the man. [23] The man said, "This is now bone of my bones and flesh of my flesh; she shall be called 'woman,' for she was taken out of man."

[24] That is why a man leaves his father and mother and is united to his wife, and they become one flesh.

[25] Adam and his wife were both naked, and they felt no shame.

A RENEWED LIFE

2 Corinthians 5:17 provides a reminder of the immediate transformation that took place in our lives at salvation. "If anyone is in Christ, he is a new creation; the old has gone, the new has come!" You are alive in Christ. Your spirit is restored. You have a new hope and a new life! Read those wonderful statements again. Is there something in your mind that makes you want to say "but…." Maybe you want to believe, but it's such a struggle to walk in the promise of God's freedom because of that thing… you know, something that you did, or didn't do… that conversation… that burst of anger. Maybe it wasn't a single incident but a season of your life when you walked away from God. Memories of past failures, condemnation and fear can dominate your thinking and limit our ability to live in the liberty that God has provided for you through Christ. So, ponder this – Eve was created with no shame. This week we will look at the reality, plan and promise for all those born again through faith in Jesus. His promise is one of renewal, fullness, and open invitation for you to leave your past behind and journey with Him in a renewed life.

SESSION QUESTIONS

—

WEEK FOUR

DAY 01   Read through Psalm 103 completely. Summarize what this passage tells you about God's attitude toward the sins of those who are His children.

DAY 02   Read back through Psalm 103 again today. What new elements of God's love stick out to you? Write out verses 10-13 on a card and post it in a prominent place. Take the rest of the week to commit them to memory.

DAY 03   Turn to Isaiah 41:18-20. How have you experienced God's promise of restoration? Specifically think about areas of your life that could once be described as a "wasteland" and how they may be flourishing now. Notice why God brings about these kinds of transformations. (vs 20)

DAY 04   Look up Isaiah 54:1-5 & Joel 2:21-27 to read God's message to wayward Israel, paying special attention to the words of restoration and removal of shame. Apply what you read to yourself.

DAY 05   Read through Psalm 32. In your journal, write down specific things that still cause shame and guilt. In a different color pen, write Psalm 32:1 over the top of your list and begin today to accept the full forgiveness of God.

WEEK
FIVE

FEMININE HEART

A SUITABLE HELPER

—

GENESIS 2:15-18

[15] The Lord God took the man and put him in the Garden of Eden to work it and take care of it. [16] And the Lord God commanded the man, "You are free to eat from any tree in the garden; [17] but you must not eat from the tree of the knowledge of good and evil, for when you eat from it you will certainly die." [18] The Lord God said, "It is not good for the man to be alone. I will make a helper suitable for him."

—

For this section, choose one of the three options to continue reading and answering session questions on:

     A *singleness* (p. 34-35)

     B *marriage* (p. 36-37)

     C *motherhood* (p. 38-39)

A

singleness

Relationships for us who aren't married can be… well... complicated, right? There's that part of you that's independent and can take care of yourself. You've proved it dozens of times, and you don't need anyone to help. But there's another part that desperately longs for companionship, interaction and assistance of other people. Some days you feel confident and certain, and then there are those other days where you may not be so sure. As Christian singles, we know that our primary relationship should be vertical: with God the Father, through Jesus, dependent on the Holy Spirit, but we also relate horizontally to others as well. Genesis 2 describes how God designed us as women from the beginning. This week we'll back up to examine God's original plan to get a sharper picture of our role as helpers, and for the remainder of the session, look at what Scripture has to say to us who are not married. A clear understanding of what God says lays the foundation for how we can learn to walk in the fullness of who we are in Christ regardless of our marital status.

SESSION QUESTIONS

—

WEEK FIVE

DAY 01
Eve was designed by God to be a helper to Adam, and since she was created to perfectly reflect this aspect of God's nature, "helper" is part of the DNA for all women. But instead of being a position of servitude that is "less than," it's an exalted position of crucial importance. To better understand what God intended this role to be, take a look at Genesis 2:18. The Hebrew word translated for "helper" is "ezer" (pronounced AY-ZER). Look up other passages that use this word (Deut. 33:26, 29; Psalm 33:20, 70:5, 115:9-11, 121:1-2; Hosea 13:9). Who is the "ezer" in these passages and what kind of help is needed/delivered? Write down your thoughts about how this challenges your understanding of what it means to be "ezer"?

DAY 02
The Greek word for "helper" is "boethos," meaning "to render urgent aid." Answer the questions from yesterday for Matt. 15:25; Mark 9:22; Acts 16:9; 2 Cor. 6:2; Heb. 2:18, 13:6. Realizing through your study that God designates Himself to be "ezer" and "boethos" of His people, reread Genesis 2:18-24. Summarize how you might fulfill the role of "vital helper" to the people closest to you.

DAY 03
Paul's first letter to the Corinthian church was written in response to the many questions new believers had about how to live as Christ followers. This is why the chapters sometimes seem to jump from topic to topic to include things like church discipline, giving, the Lord's supper and the gifts of the Spirit. It's in this context that the Apostle writes the main New Testament passage that speaks directly to the subject of singleness. To get the full context of these verses, read the entire 7th chapter of 1 Corinthians, focusing on what is said specifically to single people. Journal your initial thoughts.

DAY 04
The Bible doesn't say specifically whether Paul was ever married (many scholars believe he never was), but it's clear that he didn't have a wife at the time of the writing of 1 Corinthians. With that in mind, read 7:7. Notice that he describes marital status, married or single, as a gift. How can you view your current status in life in this way? In what ways can it be offered back to God as an offering? Be specific as how this relates to you.

DAY 05
Paul uses the phrase "undivided devotion" at the end of verses 32-35. Regardless of your marital state or what "concerns" occupy your thinking each day, how can you cultivate a single-minded devotion to the Lord even in the midst of every day responsibilities?

marriage

Ahh… your wedding day! That wonderful moment in time when your forever family was born. A new chapter in your life. The binding of two hearts, two lives, two loves into one.

And then, married life began. You may have found (possibly quickly) that it doesn't always look like what you imagined back before you said "I do." The wonderful moments of love and happiness in the arms of your beloved will also come with frustration, conflict and misunderstanding because you are two imperfect humans living as one. You most likely love the romance side, but some days all you want is for him to pick up his socks and start the dishwasher without being asked. The question lingers: How can living with this man that I love so much be so difficult?

Women, by nature, are relational. It's one of the key ways we reflect the image of God. While we need to make our relationship with Jesus our primary focus, we also need to learn how to live out that spiritual relationship with the people that are closest to us. And who is closer than the one you sleep beside, share the tube of toothpaste with and hold hands with when you are afraid?

But… often when you get close to someone, especially your husband, the rough edges that you both have scrape against each other. When that happens, the default thinking is often: "If only he would change, then everything would be better…"

While it's probably true that your guy has some areas that can improve, it's not a wife's job entirely to point out the flaws in her husband, but rather to bring our view of self (we'll get to that next session) and our role as wives that in line with God's Word. This week we'll look at God's design for women that's revealed in the creation of Eve and work to build an understanding of what it means to be a companion and helper to your "one and only."

SESSION QUESTIONS

—

DAY 01
Eve was designed by God to be a helper to Adam and since she was created to perfectly reflect this aspect of God's nature, "helper" is part the DNA for all women, but instead of being a position of servitude that is "less than," it's an exalted position of crucial importance. To better understand what God intended the role to be, take a look at Genesis 2:18. The Hebrew word for "helper" is "ezer" (pronounced AY-ZER and most often translated 'help or helper') Look up other passages that use this word (Deut. 33:26, 29; Psalm 33:20, 70:5, 115:9-11, 121:1-2; Hosea 13:9) Who is the "ezer" in these passages and what kind of help is needed/delivered? Write down your thoughts about how this changes your understanding of Eve's designation as "ezer" to Adam?

DAY 02
The Greek word for "helper" is "boethos" meaning "to render urgent aid." Answer the questions from yesterday for Matt. 15:25; Mark 9:22; Acts 16:9; 2 Cor. 6:2; Heb. 2:18, 13:6. Realizing through your study that God designates Himself to be "ezer" and "boethos" of His people, reread Genesis 2:18-24. Summarize what you learned that impacts the understanding of your calling from Him to be "helper."

DAY 03
Turn over to Ephesians 5:21-33 to read some familiar verses about wives and husbands. Setting aside any previous ideas about this passage, read it with freshness. What is Paul saying about the purpose of marriage?

DAY 04
What are your initial thoughts about the word "submission"? Read Ephesians 5:21-33 again. Thinking about what Christ did for the Church (you), in what new way can you understand what Paul meant? How does your role in marriage become a joy and not an obligation when it emulates verse 31?

DAY 05
Often people think Paul used marriage to illustrate the relationship between Christ and the church. But if you flip the understanding around, what new vision for your marriage can you adopt if the unity of Christ and the Church is the model for marriage?

motherhood

—

¹³ Then the Lord God said to the woman, "What is this you have done?" The woman said, "The serpent deceived me, and I ate." ¹⁴ So the Lord God said to the serpent, "Because you have done this, "Cursed are you above all livestock and all wild animals! You will crawl on your belly and you will eat dust all the days of your life. ¹⁵ And I will put enmity between you and the woman, and between your offspring and hers; he will crush your head, and you will strike his heel." ¹⁶ To the woman he said, "I will make your pains in childbearing very severe; with painful labor you will give birth to children.

Your desire will be for your husband, and he will rule over you." ¹⁷ To Adam he said, "Because you listened to your wife and ate fruit from the tree about which I commanded you, 'You must not eat from it,' "Cursed is the ground because of you; through painful toil you will eat food from it all the days of your life. ¹⁸ It will produce thorns and thistles for you, and you will eat the plants of the field.¹⁹ By the sweat of your brow you will eat your food until you return to the ground, since from it you were taken; for dust you are and to dust you will return." ²⁰ Adam named his wife Eve because she would become the mother of all the living.

Our world seems so vastly unlike the one in which Eve lived. Her lush and perfect Garden had no cell phones demanding attention, no social media outbursts, no generational family squabbles, no irrational bosses or nosey neighbors, and no news reports to spark flashpoints of fear, distress and confusion. Sounds amazing, doesn't it? Today's complex society teems with such chaos and turmoil that sometimes it might seem that the best option to survive would be to barricade yourself and your children behind a steel door and just wait for Jesus to come! But instead of hiding, we can look to the Lord and find strength in perhaps an unlikely verse.

Adam named his wife Eve because she would become the mother of all the living (Gen 3:20). Notice that this announcement came after that fateful day when Eve made the most unhealthy snack choice of all time. Through her disobedience to God's one command, sin entered the world and touched off a cataclysm of corruption and deterioration that reverberated throughout time. After she and her perfect mate faced the consequences of their actions, Adam turned to his beloved companion and bestowed upon her a new designation. Once simply called "woman" (Gen. 2:23), her name would now be "Eve" … mother of all living or more succinctly, Life giver. It was a name of hope. A name of mercy. A name of grace. It reminded them that the curses which came as a result of disobedience were also embedded by God with expectation. Though death was now in the picture, the Lord had not turned His back on humanity. Life would still continue (Gen 3:20).

In Eve's new name, we who are moms (and thus, life-givers) also have hope that forms the solid foundation of faith that can sustain us and our families no matter what happens around us. We need not shrink away in fear of what's to come, nor lock our children away from the concerns of the world. Instead, as we cling to the promises of God, we can point them toward Jesus who alone will be their refuge and shelter (Is. 25:4). As believers in Christ and through the power of the Holy Spirit, we moms can confidently rely on our Savior to provide what we cannot do ourselves (2 Cor. 12:9-10). Where we are weak, He is strong. Where we fail, He succeeds. Where we have nothing, He is everything.

For the remainder of this session, we'll turn our attention to the tough but wonderful calling of motherhood. Whether you are a brand new mom to your first bundle of joy, are on the backside of parenting, or don't even have plans to be a parent, Scripture says we all have a role in mothering this generation. Let's join together to dig into the Word of God and discover grace, mercy and ample help for our time of need (Heb. 4:16).

SESSION QUESTIONS

—

WEEK FIVE

DAY 01

Life-giver. How keenly were you aware of that truth as you first felt your tiny child begin to move within your body? A few short months later, a squirming, crying new human being was place in your arms, completely dependent upon you for all his or her needs. Or maybe you gave life to your child in another way. You took a child biologically born from another, and voluntarily brought this new person into your home, made him or her your own, and began a new journey… a new life… together as a family. Care for a child's physical well-being is a vast and all-encompassing responsibility, but believing parents need to remember that it's also our job to offer ourselves as instruments of God to bring spiritual life to our children as well. Read back through the familiar passage in Eph. 2:1-3 to see the condition of all those who do not know Christ as Savior. Continue reading vs. 4-9 to be reminded of God's glorious answer to those who are dead in sin!

DAY 02

Child rearing techniques are just about as diverse as children are themselves. While we can have healthy and spirited debate around the best approaches to potty training, diet, social media, screen limits, and the many topics that are involved in raising strong, productive kids, for Christian parents, there should be unity on the ultimate goal. And the good news is that the goal is the same for them as it is for you! Read Romans 8:28-29 (NIV) to discover what you (and they) are designed for. Look it up in the Message version for another understanding of what this means.

DAY 03 Read 1 Corinthians 11:1. The English Standard Version says Paul encouraged the new believers to "imitate me" as he imitated Christ. If your children are imitating your behavior (and they will), what do they absorb from you about the importance of prayer, the Word of God and worship? What's impressed on them regarding service to God, generosity, humility and love for others? Think less about "family devotion" time, and more about what they might learn from you when you meet strangers, travel in the car together, or overhear your conversations on the phone. But don't become focused on being the "perfect" mother either. Since we all sin, make mistakes and fall short of righteousness, consider what they might learn about the Gospel when they hear you say "I'm sorry," "I was wrong" and "I forgive you." Think of some other practical things (like speaking softly, putting their interests before yours, etc) that would display an accurate picture of Christ to your children. Write these down and begin to implement one this week.

DAY 04 It's easy to get focused on external behaviors in our children and forget about the importance of internal attitudes of the heart. Look up and begin to memorize Prov. 4:23. Write this verse out and put it on your refrigerator to remind you to make your primary focus the protection, nurturing and development of a soft and pliable heart in your child that's sensitive to the Lord.

DAY 05 Think back to your years in elementary school, middle and high school. Did you make any bad mistakes, poor choices or unhealthy decisions? Sure you did! We all do! Next question: How excited were you to tell your parents about your blunders? Probably not very, right? Let's face it. Kids make mistakes, and they may not always want to confess their failures to you, but they do need a safe place to unpack their heartaches and troubles. Read Gal. 6:1-2; James 5:16 & Prov. 27:17. There is value in accountability. If your children are very young, begin now to look for godly mentors and role models. Foster relationships between them and trusted family members and friends who live for Jesus. If your children are older, encourage openness with youth leaders, spiritual mentors, upright leaders and godly adult role models. Ask God to lead you to people who can champion a life of faith in them!

FEMININE HEART

A SUITABLE HELPER

COLOSSIANS 1:1-23

[1] Paul, an apostle of Christ Jesus by the will of God, and Timothy our brother, [2] To God's holy people in Colossae, the faithful brothers and sister in Christ: Grace and peace to you from God our Father. [3] We always thank God, the Father of our Lord Jesus Christ, when we pray for you, [4] because we have heard of your faith in Christ Jesus and of the love you have for all God's people— [5] the faith and love that spring from the hope stored up for you in heaven and about which you have already heard in the true message of the gospel [6] that has come to you. In the same way, the gospel is bearing fruit and growing throughout the whole world—just as it has been doing among you since the day you heard it and truly understood God's grace. [7] You learned it from Epaphras, our dear fellow servant, who is a faithful minister of Christ on our behalf, [8] and who also told us of your love in the Spirit. [9] For this reason, since the day we heard about you, we have not stopped praying for you. We continually ask God to fill you with the knowledge of his will through all the wisdom and understanding that the Spirit gives, [10] so that you may live a life worthy of the Lord and please him in every way: bearing fruit in every good work, growing in the knowledge of God, [11] being strengthened with all power according to his glorious might so that you may have great endurance and patience, [12] and giving joyful thanks to the Father, who has qualified you to share in the inheritance of his holy people in the kingdom of light. [13] For he has rescued us from the dominion of darkness and brought us into the kingdom of the Son he loves, [14] in whom we have redemption, the forgiveness of sins. [15] The Son is the image of the invisible God, the firstborn over all creation. [16] For in him all things were created: things in heaven and on earth, visible and invisible, whether thrones

or powers or rulers or authorities; all things have been created through him and for him. [17] He is before all things, and in him all things hold together. [18] And he is the head of the body, the church; he is the beginning and the firstborn from among the dead, so that in everything he might have the supremacy. [19] For God was pleased to have all his fullness dwell in him, [20] and through him to reconcile to himself all things, whether things on earth or things in heaven, by making peace through his blood, shed on the cross.

[21] Once you were alienated from God and were enemies in your minds because of your evil behavior. [22] But now he has reconciled you by Christ's physical body through death to present you holy in his sight, without blemish and free from accusation— [23] if you continue in your faith, established and firm, and do not move from the hope held out in the gospel. This is the gospel that you heard and that has been proclaimed to every creature under heaven, and of which I, Paul, have become a servant.

The moment you trusted Jesus as your Savior, everything changed! Scripture says that your heart of stone has been replaced with a heart of flesh and that God's Spirit now lives in you! (Ez. 36:26-17) Everything on the inside is different – you have come from death to life, but what about on the outside? Well, that transformation can take a little more time, can't it? Little by little and with great patience and compassion, the Holy Spirit sifts us so that as we yield to Him we look, act and BECOME different every day. And, not just on Sunday when we're dressed in our cutest clothes and our make-up is fixed just right. The transformation that God intends needs to also show itself on our worst days when we feel bad, but we choose to love anyway, and to the people who try our patience the most, but we choose to forgive anyway. It's within our families, with husbands, children, parents and siblings where our new life in Christ is tested the most. So, let's jump in to Paul's letter to the Colossians where we're challenged to take our relationship with Christ seriously and strive to live lives that are an accurate reflection of the grace of God that we have received and which dwells within us through His Spirit.

For this section, choose one of the three options to continue answering the session questions on:

A *singleness* (p. 48-49) **B** *marriage* (p. 50-51) **C** *motherhood* (p. 52-53)

intro to Colossians

Pause for a minute and think about a special place that positively impacted you during your growing up years. Maybe you thought of the fondness you have for your childhood home, or the school where you spent so many hours practicing in the band or playing a sport, or it could be the building where you held your first job. In some cases, the physical structures may not exist any longer, but the impact of places like these live on through the influence they had on our lives. In much the same way, the ancient city of Colossae is like that. Though no one can point to it on a modern map or visit this historical place, the effect of this relatively inconsequential Middle Eastern city lives powerfully in the lives of every believer today.

Early in its history, Colossae was one of a triad of important cities located east of the Mediterranean in the area where Turkey now exists. It was a large commercial location that was chiefly known for its wool production and manufacture of a purple dye made from a native flower. Later, during the time of the Roman Empire, new trade routes were established that bypassed Colossae, diverting the bulk of travelers and merchants through Laodicea, ten miles to the north. Due to the change in traffic, one city became rich and prosperous while the other suffered decline. The destruction of the once great gathering place came only a short time after Paul wrote his epistle (around 60 AD) when Colossae was struck by an earthquake that demolished most of the structures. Though a small group continued to dwell there for a time, it was never rebuilt and eventually deteriorated completely, leaving only ruins that, to date, have not been excavated. While nothing remains of the actual city today, its most enduring legacy continues to dwell in the hearts of believers around the world in the form of the

beloved book of Colossians. Though Paul never personally visited this church, his friend and Colossian church founder, Epaphras (1:7), contacted him in a Roman prison to seek advice about how to counter the arguments of false teachers who infiltrated the church, rejected the divinity of Jesus Christ, and sought to lead the early believers into heresy.

In his letter of response, Paul uses some of the most lofty and excellent language in the entire New Testament to expound upon the supremacy of Jesus Christ over all things (1:15-17). Because of His divinity and the authority given to Him by the Father, Jesus rightfully holds the position as head over the church (1:18) and through His sacrifice on the cross, reconciled all things to Himself (1:19-20), making believers alive to God and setting them on the path to right living (1:21-23, 3:1-25). This proper view of Christ served to be the remedy for the troubles facing the early church and continues to provide a solid foundation for our Christian life today.

As we move into this study of the more practical aspects of our lives, it's imperative that we cultivate and maintain this same viewpoint of Christ and filter all our decisions through His authority and preeminence. When the world around seeks to confuse us with an earthly and temporary view of relationships, marriage, parenting, work, adversity, faith, etc, it is our knowledge of the truth anchored in scripture that gives meaning and purpose to our lives and assists us in developing a God-centered mission mindset that helps us willingly yield ourselves to Jesus through our words and ultimately our whole lives.

A

singleness

SESSION QUESTIONS

—

WEEK SIX

DAY 01 The remainder of this session will focus on questions surrounding singleness, but remember that "unmarried" doesn't mean "alone." You have family, friends, and close relationships and how you see yourself and interact with others will be strongly affected by a renewed understanding of the supremacy of Jesus and your relationship to Him. Read the passage at the beginning of this session, meditating on what it says about Christ and about you. Then find your Bible and continue reading chapter 2. Make 2 columns on a piece of paper and spend a few minutes filling one side with everything you learn about Christ from this passage.

DAY 02 Go back through the chapters from yesterday. In the second column, list anything you learn about yourself or how God intends for you to live. For example, in Christ, God sees me as holy and faithful (1:2); God intends for me to live a life worthy of the Lord (1:10).

DAY 03 Write down any initial thoughts regarding your attitude about being a single person. (For example, I enjoy being single. I am lonely sometimes. I worry about having someone to help take care of me in the future, etc.) Read Col. 3:1-17. How should your attitudes be affected by what you've read in Colossians so far?

DAY 04 Go slowly through verses 3:1-4. What's the difference between setting your heart (vs 1) and your mind (vs 2) on things above? Why do you think Paul included both? As a single person, what things are your heart and mind set on other than God?

DAY 05 Verses 3 & 4 challenge us to adopt an eternal perspective and set it as ruler over all we think and do. What difference would it make in how you lived if you refocused the desires of your mind and heart on the things of God?

B

marriage

SESSION QUESTIONS

—

WEEK SIX

DAY 01 The remainder of this session will focus in on your relationship with your husband, but that will first be strongly affected by a renewed understanding of the supremacy of Jesus and your relationship to Him. Read the passage at the beginning of this session, meditating on what it says about Christ and about you. Then find your Bible and continue reading through chapter 2. Make 2 columns on a piece of paper and spend a few minutes filling one side with everything you learn about Christ from this passage.

DAY 02 Go back through the chapters from yesterday. In the other column, list anything you learn about yourself or how God intends for you to live. For example, in Christ, God sees me as holy and faithful (1:2); God intends for me to live a life worthy of the Lord (1:10).

DAY 03 We will spend most of the next three weeks focusing on the instructions in Col. 3:1-17 and work to apply them specifically to our marriages. Read this passage today. Write down any initial thoughts regarding your relationship with your husband, especially include how it might be impacted by what you learned/wrote from earlier in the week.

DAY 04 Go slowly through verses 3:1-4. What's the difference between setting your heart (vs 1) and your mind (vs 2) on things above? Why do you think Paul included both?

DAY 05 Verses 3 & 4 challenge us to adopt an eternal perspective and set it as ruler over all we think and do. What difference would it make in your marriage if you refocused the desires of your mind and heart on the things of God?

C

motherhood

SESSION QUESTIONS

—

WEEK SIX

DAY 01 Scripture clearly gives the responsibility for spiritual training to parents, and even if we can't give them everything materially that we'd like for them to have, we can still extraordinarily outfit them for life by helping them know and follow Jesus. But that can only happen if we as parents are following Jesus first. Read through Colossian 1. Focus in on verses 15-23. Have you recognized Jesus as the "image of the invisible God," and as Ruler, Creator and Sustainer of "all things?" Has your faith in Christ's blood reconciled you to God and made it possible for you to have peace with Him? If so, take a fresh look at your own story of faith. In your journal write out some key points and thank Jesus for all that He has done for, through, and in you. ****If you haven't asked Jesus to take away your sin, then you can do that right now. Read John 3:1-18; and Rom. 10:9-10. Call your mentor to ask any questions about salvation or what it means to follow Jesus.*

DAY 02 Look up Deuteronomy 6:1-9. (Jesus quoted verse 5 in Matthew 22:34-40 identifying this as the greatest commandment.) Think about what it means to love God with all of your heart, soul, and strength. How are each of those elements different? What's the meaning of the verse when you put the pieces all together?

DAY 03 Go back to Deuteronomy 6:6-7 and look it up in the NASB version. What does it mean for the commandments of God to be "on your heart"? Noticing the pronoun in the next sentence, to whom is this command given? While instruction can be assisted by the church, teachers, pastors and others, the primary responsibility for spiritual training is given to parents and should be incorporated into all our activities. Think carefully about how verse 7 is completely dependent on verse 5 & 6. Write down your thoughts.

Continue in Deuteronomy 6 again today, by reading verses 8-9. The Pharisees used to take these verses very literally by crafting small boxes (called phylacteries) to hold verses of Scripture which they tied on their foreheads and hands with leather straps. Obviously, that isn't the intent of this passage. If you consider "hands" to be symbolic of our activities, and the "forehead" a symbol for our thoughts, what do you think this verse now means? How will displaying "love for God" in those ways impact what you read in verse 7?

Return to Colossians 1:9-14. With all that you learned this week in mind, insert your child's name into this passage and make it a personal prayer that you pray for him or her. (For example … "asking God to fill "Mary/John" with the knowledge of His will…") If you have more than one child, then pray this passage for each of them on successive days of the week. Begin to use this pattern prayer on their behalf regularly.

Read Colossians 2 this weekend.

FEMININE HEART

COLOSSIANS 3:1-11

[1] Since, then, you have been raised with Christ, set your hearts on things above, where Christ is, seated at the right hand of God. [2] Set your minds on things above, not on earthly things. [3] For you died, and your life is now hidden with Christ in God. [4] When Christ, who is your life, appears, then you also will appear with him in glory. [5] Put to death, therefore, whatever belongs to your earthly nature: sexual immorality, impurity, lust, evil desires and greed, which is idolatry. [6] Because of these, the wrath of God is coming.

[7] You used to walk in these ways, in the life you once lived. [8] But now you must also rid yourselves of all such things as these: anger, rage, malice, slander, and filthy language from your lips. [9] Do not lie to each other, since you have taken off your old self with its practices [10] and have put on the new self, which is being renewed in knowledge in the image of its Creator. [11] Here there is no Gentile or Jew, circumcised or uncircumcised, barbarian, Scythian, slave or free, but Christ is all, and is in all.

———

For this section, choose one of the three options to continue reading and answering session questions on:

A *singleness* *(p. 56-57)*

B *marriage* *(p. 58-59)*

C *motherhood* *(p. 60-61)*

A

singleness

SESSION QUESTIONS

—

WEEK SEVEN

DAY 01   In this week's verses, Paul begins instructing us in how to live. How do verses 5-11 relate to verses 1-4? Consider how that foundation gives new motivation for (and power to affect) behavior change.

DAY 02   This section contains a list of many of the ways that may have characterized the life you once lived before beginning a relationship with Jesus. In a spirit of prayer and honesty, consider which one(s) of these still influence your actions and attitudes. Widen your thinking to include anything in your past that is still present in your life that Paul didn't specifically mention.

DAY 03   Sexuality is an area of concern for many Christian singles. The world proliferates so much error about this topic that it's essential to establish a Biblical framework to guide decision making about this important area of our lives. Look up and make notes about these verses: Col. 3:5; 1 Cor. 6:12-20; Gal. 5:13-18; 1 Thes. 4:1-8; 1 Peter 2:9-12; 2 Tim. 2:22.

DAY 04   If you struggle in the area of sexual purity, there is forgiveness and wholeness available to you. Read John 8:1-11. What Jesus said to this woman, He also says to you. With the guidance of the Holy Spirit, make a plan that will help you begin walking in holiness. (See 1 Cor. 10:13; 1 John 1:9) Remember that your mentor is a safe place to discuss these concerns.

DAY 05   Conclude this week of study by reading Ephesians 4:17-24. Think about the drastic difference between Paul's description of the former way of living and that of one who has become a believer. Is that radical change evident to those who know you? What needs to change so that others can see Christ in you?

B

marriage

SESSION QUESTIONS

—

WEEK SEVEN

DAY 01   In this week's verses, Paul begins instructing us how to live as believers in Jesus. How do verses 5-11 relate to verses 1-4? Consider how that foundation gives new motivation for (and power to affect) behavior change.

DAY 02   This section contains a list of many of the ways that may have characterized the life you once lived before beginning a relationship with Jesus. In a spirit of prayer and honesty, consider which one(s) of these still influence your marriage. Widen your thinking to include anything from your past that presently influences your life/marriage that Paul didn't specifically mention.

DAY 03   It's easy to point to others as being at fault for the struggles we encounter in relationships. While still keeping in mind the exercise from yesterday, consider what would change in your relationship with your husband if you seriously began to do what Paul instructed in verse 7-8. (Look up Eph. 5:1-10)

DAY 04   In verses 8-10, Paul challenges believers to stop activity that divides and because of our relationship to Christ, engage in activity that binds people together. Thinking about how you relate to your husband, what do you need to adjust? (Think about how he might answer that question as well.) What new actions/habits/attitudes can you institute to encourage a stronger sense of unity? Be specific.

DAY 05   Even though couples may be together for a significant period of time, husbands and wives can still have differing opinions based on background, interests, leisure activities, work, etc. Make a general list of things on which you and your husband have divergent opinions. Read back through the verses for this week, focusing in on verse 11 to see what Paul said about differences between people. How should knowing "Christ is all and is in all" change your attitude when you disagree on issues? How can you celebrate your husband's differences?

(C)

motherhood

SESSION QUESTIONS

—

WEEK SEVEN

DAY 01
"God will never give you more than you can handle." Besides being a flatly unbiblical statement [1 Cor. 10:13 actually says God will not give you more temptation than you can bear], any mother will tell you that the sentiment in itself is near lunacy. Think about it. You are charged with the responsibility for the spiritual, mental, emotional, financial and physical development, care and training of this human being…. for at least the next eighteen years! (Mothers with grown children will attest that concern over, involvement with, and prayers for your children do not end when they move out!) When you multiply this responsibility by 2, or 4, or more, of course, you can't handle that. No one could! But the wonderful truth is that Jesus never expects you to carry this responsibility alone. Read through Col. 3:1-4. Concentrate on verse 4. What do you think it means for Christ to be your life? How should that play out in a practical, every day way?

DAY 02
The Holy Spirit lives in all those who believe in Jesus. Read through John 14:15-27 to see what Jesus said about the job of the Spirit. What encouragement does this give you as you face the tasks and complexities of raising your child(ren)?

DAY 03
Read back through the passage from yesterday. Focus in on verse 18. Considering your role as protective, nurturing mother, how does that change your understanding of Christ's promise to not leave you as an orphan? Write down any emotions you feel as a result of this assurance.

DAY 04
Even though you might have a husband, parents, siblings or friends as support, it's easy to feel alone as a mother. Look up Isaiah 41:13-14 for an everlasting reminder. Come back to this passage several times today.

DAY 05
The world, the flesh, and the devil are our constant enemies as believers in Christ. What they mean for evil, God can always turn to good. Widen out your reading from yesterday to include verses 11-20. Pick out and think about the section that speaks most to you where you are.

SESSION ONE / WEEK EIGHT

WEEK
EIGHT

FEMININE HEART

COLOSSIANS 3:12-14

[12] Therefore, as God's chosen people, holy and dearly loved, clothe yourselves with compassion, kindness, humility, gentleness and patience. [13] Bear with each other and forgive one another if any of you has a grievance against someone. Forgive as the Lord forgave you. [14] And over all these virtues put on love, which binds them all together in perfect unity.

———

For this section, choose one of the three options to continue reading and answering session questions on:

A *singleness* (p. 64-65)

B *marriage* (p. 66-67)

C *motherhood* (p. 68-69)

A

singleness

SESSION QUESTIONS

—

WEEK EIGHT

DAY 01 Unmarried, divorced and widowed people can struggle with feelings of loneliness, and rejection. For believers, value and worth does not come from any earthly relationship, but is given to us by Christ. Read Col. 3:12-14. Before focusing on what this passage says to do, first begin reflecting on what it means to be "chosen," "holy" and "dearly loved" by God. Make notes on this and what Jesus says about you in John 15:1-17.

DAY 02 Turn to Isaiah 43:1-7. Read it as God's personal message to you. Give special attention to verse 4.

DAY 03 Use your Bible app or a computer to look up 1 John 3:1-2 in the NIV. Grab a dictionary to get a good definition of the word "lavish" and in your journal, reflect on the manner in which God loves you.

DAY 04 Flip back to Ephesians 1 to find another appearance of the word "lavish." What is lavished this time? Add some notes to yesterday's entry about the extravagant heart of God toward you. How can this help in times when you feel alone or rejected?

DAY 05 End this week back in Col. 3:12-14. How should embracing the truth of being "chosen and dearly loved" translate in to your relationships with others? Making note of what Paul specifically said in this passage, how can you practically express holy love to others outside the context of marriage?

B

marriage

SESSION QUESTIONS

—

WEEK EIGHT

DAY 01 — This section of Colossians 3 contains more instruction on living in relationship with others. Before you get to specifics, reflect on what it means to be "chosen," "holy" and "dearly loved" by God. Make notes on this and what Jesus says about you in John 15:9-17.

DAY 02 — Go through this section again, considering what it means to "clothe yourself" with the virtues listed in vs 12. Is that any different from just simply being kind, gentle, patient, etc? How can you "wear" these virtues in the moments when you feel irritated and frustrated with your husband?

DAY 03 — Read the section again. Make notes on what it means to "bear with" your husband. Cross reference Ephesians 4:1-3 to see "how" to bear with others.

DAY 04 — Start by looking up a definition for the word "grievance." What real or imagined offenses have piled up in your marriage? Notice the "and" in the middle of Col. 3:13. Can you really have one without the other? Why are both elements necessary to strengthen your marriage?

DAY 05 — Read verse 13 & 14 together. In thinking about how "the Lord forgave you," how were His actions bound together in love? Remember that this was His attitude toward you before you sought or asked for forgiveness. How can Christ's example change your interaction when you have "grievances" with your husband? Be practical in seeing areas where this can be applied.

C

motherhood

SESSION QUESTIONS

—

WEEK EIGHT

DAY 01

Begin by reading this week's section of Colossians. Notice how Paul connects God's attitude of love and acceptance of you with the instruction to "clothe yourself" with His virtues. Why do you think that's necessary? What difference does/should it make in your interaction with others (specifically your children) to first know that you are "chosen" and "dearly loved?"

DAY 02

Read back through the passage from yesterday, but this time think about your children. When our kids make us angry, sometimes we can forget that they are dearly loved by the Lord. Read Psalm 127 as a reminder of God's attitude toward the little (and not so little) ones He gave to you.

DAY 03

Do you struggle to contain your emotions in the heat of the moment? Is anger a reoccurring problem? These can be issues that are difficult to control, but you can through Christ. Look up Romans 7:14-25 to get insight into Paul's own struggle with sin … and its solution (vs 24-25)! Continue reading through chapter 8, verse 11 for how a Spirit-controlled mind is a crucial part of the solution (vs 5-6). How could reordering your thoughts according to Phil. 4:8 help diffuse volatile situations? When emotions begin to escalate, learn to take a personal "time-out" to give yourself the chance to change your thinking.

DAY 04

The discussion of discipline in child rearing can bring out strong differences of opinion. While we can disagree on how, when and why correction is needed, believers must remember that at its core, discipline is an expression of love from God. Read Hebrews 12:5-11. From this passage, what can you discern about the motivation behind discipline? First apply what it says to yourself as a child of God, then think about your children. What does it say about our attitude when we fail to discipline our children?

Are you sick of picking up toys? Is fatigue setting in from yet another school project? Ever feel like making and cleaning up one more meal just might make you snap? It's easy to get caught up in the demands of everyday life and lose sight of what really matters for eternity. Look up Psalm 39:4-7. Remember that the days of diapers and sticky hands will end. As will the days of term papers and playoff games. When those temporary things are in the past, what enduring impression do you want to remain on your children? Write out a statement that will help you maintain this eternal focus as you navigate the demands of life right now.

FEMININE HEART

COLOSSIANS 3:15-17

[15] Let the peace of Christ rule in your hearts, since as members of one body you were called to peace. And be thankful. [16] Let the message of Christ dwell among you richly as you teach and admonish one another with all wisdom through psalms, hymns, and songs from the Spirit, singing to God with gratitude in your hearts. [17] And whatever you do, whether in word or deed, do it all in the name of the Lord Jesus, giving thanks to God the Father through him.

—

For this section, choose one of the three options to continue reading and answering session questions on:

A *singleness (p. 72-73)*

B *marriage (p. 74-75)*

C *motherhood (p. 76-77)*

A

singleness

SESSION QUESTIONS

—

WEEK NINE

DAY 01 Since all the responsibilities for living (health care, child rearing, budgeting, investments, monthly expenses, etc.) fall completely on the shoulders of you as a single person, it's easy to become worried and anxious. Thinking about your specific situation, how can you practically "let the peace of Christ rule in your heart?" (vs 15) How does thankfulness play a part in dissipating anxiety?

DAY 02 Often believers find it difficult to be thankful and praise God when things don't happen the way we think they should. Read Psalm 143, thinking about how David approached God in difficult times. How is his attitude different than your response to heartache, frustration and disappointment? Specifically apply this to any struggles you have with being single.

DAY 03 Much of our time as singles is given to occupation. Considering the work you do every day, move back to the passage in Colossians 3 and focus in on verse 17. What practical alterations in your mental attitude or physical routine will enable you to accomplish "whatever you do" in the name of the Lord Jesus? Memorize this verse.

DAY 04 Look for the phrase "whatever you do" in the remainder of Colossians 3. Makes notes on how these instructions can help you in fulfilling your passion for a purpose greater than yourself.

DAY 05 Wrap up this session by reading Colossians 4. Notice Paul's emphasis on prayer and think about how it should impact your priorities regardless of your marital status. Conclude this session by answering this question: How are you maximizing your God-given purpose during this season of your life?

B

marriage

SESSION QUESTIONS

—

WEEK NINE

DAY 01 In connection with your marriage and family, make a list of the things that cause you to worry. Look at Colossians 3:15. How can you practically "let the peace of Christ rule in your heart?" How does thankfulness play a part in dissipating our anxiety?

DAY 02 Often believers find it difficult to be thankful and praise God when things don't happen the way we think they should. Read Psalm 143, thinking about how David approached God in difficult times. How is his attitude different than your response to heartache, frustration and disappointment? Specifically apply this to your marriage.

DAY 03 Considering the work you do every day at home, for your husband, on your job, with children, etc, move back to the passage in Colossians 3 and focus on verse 17. Think of practical alterations in your mental attitude or physical routine that will enable you to accomplish "whatever you do" in the name of the Lord Jesus. Memorize this verse.

DAY 04 Look for the phrase "whatever you do" in the remainder of Colossians 3. Make notes on how these instructions can help you in fulfilling your passion for a purpose greater than yourself.

DAY 05 Wrap up this session by reading Colossians 4. Noticing Paul's emphasis on prayer, think about how that should impact your priorities regardless of your marital status. Conclude this session by answering this question: How are you maximizing your God-given purpose during this season of your life?

C

motherhood

S E S S I O N   Q U E S T I O N S

—

W E E K   N I N E

DAY 01 — Begin by reading the section of Colossians 3 for this week. Focus in on the instruction to "let the peace of Christ rule in your heart." How can you help foster such an attitude during times when there is turmoil or chaos in your home? Cross reference Galatians 5:22. Note what comes before and after the word "peace" in the list. Is there any significance in that? Write down your thoughts.

DAY 02 — What's your greatest fear for your child? Are you concerned about accidents, sickness, stranger-danger, influence of friends or social pressures, etc? Turn to Philippians 4:6-7 (NIV) to see what you are to do with these fears. Think about the difference between prayer, petition and thanksgiving. How much thanksgiving do you incorporate into the time you spend talking to God about these things? Try adding it a little more for the next few weeks. Note any changes in the tone of how you pray and if/when you begin to experience peace surrounding these issues. Memorize these verses.

DAY 03 — It's tempting to trust in what you can see rather than in God, who you cannot see. Look up Psalm 146:1-4. In what "prince" or "human being" are you most prone to trust? (ex. leaders, spouse, friends - don't forget to consider how you might be tempted trust yourself as well.) Note what this Psalm says about their/your ability. Apply this to your concern about your children.

DAY 04 — The alternative to trusting in flesh and blood is stated in the last half of the passage from yesterday. As you read all of Psalm 146, think about what it means to have faith in God even in the midst of legitimate concerns about life and/or the future of your children. Turn to Hebrews 11:1-2 for a reminder of the biblical definition of faith. Make notes about what faith is and isn't.

Wrap up this session by reading the rest of Colossians 3 & 4. What can you apply to your specific situation from the rules for Christian households that Paul gives to wives, husbands, fathers, children, slaves and masters? Take special note of the comprehensive instructions in vs. 23-24. Continue looking for application in 4:2-6. As you close this session of FLOURISH, go back through your notes. Write down your biggest "take-away." Conclude this session by answering this question: How are you maximizing your God-given purpose during this season of your life?

II

WHOLE & HOLY

Healthy. What comes to mind when you hear that word? Is it exercise or diet? Maybe how you feel or how you look. The word healthy might make you think of physical or mental health. For some of us, it can even conjure up feelings of defeat or hopelessness. It may be at the top of your priority list or something you rarely think about. Like everything else, the world has put its stamp on "well-being" and offers up a number of different ways for us to approach good health. So many options in fact that we often give up before we even begin.

For believers there's an added dimension to the discussion around health. Deep down we recognize we have one body, one life, and we want to maximize that life the best we can to honor God. Therefore, we need to take care of ourselves – spirit, soul, and body. In this session, we're going to come around the idea of being healthy and dig into God's Word and listen to what He has to say on the topic. His Word is above all other opinions so let's listen and learn with open hearts and fresh eyes.

1 Thessalonians 5:23-24 in The Message says:

May God himself, the God who makes everything holy and whole, make you holy and whole, put you together—spirit, soul, and body—and keep you fit for the coming of our Master, Jesus Christ. The One who called you is completely dependable. If he said it, he'll do it!

Holy and whole – spirit, soul, and body! We are made up of spirit, soul and body. All three are intricately connected, influencing one another and resulting in the whole you. How awesome to know that God wants to be directly involved in you pursuing life in every facet of who you are. The Holy Spirit leads our spirit, our spirit influences our soul, and our soul directly influences our body and physical health. And the pattern repeats. <u>Caring for ourselves</u>

spiritually, mentally and emotionally, and physically is all part of our pursuit of holiness.

Being holy, healthy, and whole is an invitation to participate, through the choices we make, to ignite the life available to us. What a gift! Every day we have an opportunity to show reverence and honor to God by how we <u>nurture ourselves</u> – not just by spending fifteen minutes alone with God, but with our whole being spirit, soul, and body. It's important to acknowledge up front that we can't just expect God to move in and make everything right for us. We have been given free will. We have a responsibility to take part in this pursuit of holiness. Jesus will be faithful to walk with us as we do the work to see ourselves experience life in greater measure under the banner of Whole and Holy, with the goal of His glory and the benefit of our good.

This is a journey and there is grace for every step and misstep. In this session we will look at spirit, soul, and body. We'll take time to learn about each of these unique areas and how we can pursue health according to the Word. As you pull on your spiritual running shoes, and maybe your physical running shoes, too, begin to ready yourself to pursue a healthier you. Let's begin by asking the Father to take you beyond what we cover in this session and lead you personally into greater depths of wholeness and holiness for your life and for His glory! For each of us, the journey will look drastically different, but God's desire is for us to love Him with our whole selves. Let's get started.

1 THESSALONIANS

Our key Scripture for Whole and Holy comes from 1 Thessalonians 5. The book of 1 Thessalonians is written by Paul to the new believers in Thessalonica. Throughout the book of Thessalonians, Paul challenges the believers to live in anticipation of Jesus coming again and to pursue holiness as they wait for His return. He warns them of false teachings and desires to inspire them to continue to grow in godliness – the result of consistently walking in the power of God's Spirit.

1 Thessalonians applies to our lives as well. The beautiful, living hope we all have in knowing that Jesus is coming again, and that we have eternal life because of Him, encourages the pursuit of being whole and holy. When our lives are finished here, or if He returns before that time, we can know we have maximized every breath He gave us to steward and honor Him well with how we lived! At the end of each week, we will spend time reading through a portion of 1 Thessalonians to keep in context with the heartbeat of all we are studying each day.

SESSION GOALS

WHOLE & HOLY

GOALS

- To embrace a new definition of what it means to be "healthy."
- To understand how spirit, soul and body are interdependent.
- To see how a relationship with Jesus can establish and/or alter our 'healthy living' goals.
- To help us see service and worship of God as the new motivation for spiritual, emotional and physical health.

QUESTIONS

- Define what it means to be healthy? How should that definition be different for you as a believer?
- What are your healthy goals for your body? What about for your soul? Spirit?
- Which is most difficult for you? Why?
- Why is focusing on just physical fitness not enough to achieve true health? Is the same true when it comes to focusing only on emotional or spiritual health?

WHOLE & HOLY

THE WAY OF WORSHIP

—

PSALM 103

SPIRIT, SOUL & BODY

For the first few weeks we'll be leaning into the spiritual expression of life. As mentioned in the intro, the Holy Spirit leads our spirit, our spirit influences our soul, and our soul directly influences our body and physical health. This is where it all starts ~ the pursuit of your relationship with Jesus. Everything flows out of this, everything issues forth from your relationship with Him and how you invest in this daily. Our relationship with Jesus will directly impact every ounce of who we are. Over the next 3 weeks we will look at developing habits that can deepen and grow our relationship with God. Through FLOURISH, we're already working on the daily discipline of studying the Word so we'll be adding a focus on worship, being still, and fasting to help us draw closer to Jesus.

—

We're kicking off our first week of whole and holy with worship. Our worship of God encompasses all of life. Pastor Louie Giglio of Passion City Church teaches that "worship is our response, both personal and corporate, to God – for who He is, and for what He's done. Expressed in the things we say and the way we live." All of who we are ~ spirit, soul, and body ~ can and should express worship to Him. This week, we will sit in some truths about worshiping God and be encouraged and inspired to express His worship to even greater measure in all we do. Our goal is to live a life of worship, so allow these truths to build a foundation for our lives.

P S A L M   1 0 3

[1] Praise the Lord, my soul; all my inmost being, praise his holy name. [2] Praise the Lord, my soul, and forget not all his benefits—[3] who forgives all your sins and heals all your diseases, [4] who redeems your life from the pit and crowns you with love and compassion, [5] who satisfies your desires with good things so that your youth is renewed like the eagle's. [6] The Lord works righteousness and justice for all the oppressed. [7] He made known his ways to Moses, his deeds to the people of Israel: [8] The Lord is compassionate and gracious, slow to anger, abounding in love. [9] He will not always accuse, nor will he harbor his anger forever; [10] he does not treat us as our sins deserve or repay us according to our iniquities. [11] For as high as the heavens are above the earth, so great is his love for those who fear him; [12] as far as the east is from the west, so far has he removed our transgressions from us.

[13] As a father has compassion on his children, so the Lord has compassion on those who fear him; [14] for he knows how we are formed, he remembers that we are dust. [15] The life of mortals is like grass, they flourish like a flower of the field; [16] the wind blows over it and it is gone, and its place remembers it no more. [17] But from everlasting to everlasting the Lord's love is with those who fear him, and his righteousness with their children's children—[18] with those who keep his covenant and remember to obey his precepts. [19] The Lord has established his throne in heaven, and his kingdom rules over all. [20] Praise the Lord, you his angels, you mighty ones who do his bidding, who obey his word. [21] Praise the Lord, all his heavenly hosts, you his servants who do his will. [22] Praise the Lord, all his works everywhere in his dominion. Praise the Lord, my soul.

SESSION QUESTIONS

—

WEEK ONE

DAY 01

Worship translates into the overflow of the heart in response to our amazing, generous, faithful, life giving God. Read Psalm 103 and note everything revealed about who God is and what He has done and will always do. We all worship something. We can easily offer up our lives and give our great-est expressions of worship to much lesser things. Take time today to write out anything that you feel competes with your worship of God and how you can redirect ALL the praise to Him.

DAY 02

Read Romans 12:1-2 in the NIV and then in The Message version. Worship may come easily when we are in a corporate worship setting, but what about our "everyday, ordinary life: eating, sleeping, going to work, and walking around life?" How are you worshiping in your everyday, not just on Sunday or in the fifteen minutes at the start of each day? Reflect in your journal on the rhythm of your day – and how you can offer all of life as worship to God?

DAY 03

Read John 4:1-30 and spend some concentrated time studying verses 21-24. Make note of what God reveals to you about a worshiper who worships in spirit and in truth. What does it mean to worship in spirit? What does it mean to worship in truth? How do both those expressions work together?

DAY 04

It's because of Jesus that you have access to the Father. Read Hebrews 10:19-22, 13:15-16. Take time to sit in the beautiful reality and gift that is yours through Jesus. God sits enthroned on high, yet you are invited to come before Him, to be in His presence with confidence! Nothing stands between you and the Father. He is fully accessible to you. Would you say you worship and pray with that confidence and freedom when approaching Him? Why or why not?

DAY 05

A heart set on Jesus is a heart at peace and filled with joy – read 1 Peter 1:3-9. The more we know Him and remain steadfast in the truth, the more He reigns in our hearts and minds. The more we know Him, the more we're moved to worship. Every day is an opportunity to pursue a life of worship. End the week by memorizing one Scripture from our study over the past 5 days – you pick!

End this week by reading 1 Thessalonians chapter 1.

WHOLE & HOLY

BE STILL AND LISTEN

be still
PSALM 46:10

be quiet
ISAIAH 30:15

wait
PSALM 27:14

listen
JEREMIAH 3:33

draw near
JAMES 4:8

These are not suggestions, but commands. All these commands require that we pull away from the craziness of life, shut out the noise, and spend time in our relationship with Jesus. On the regular! And with each command is a promise: He will draw near to us, we can hear His voice, we will have peace, find refuge, do good works, find grace….and that's just a beginning. Even knowing this hope, it can be easy to allow other things to become a priority over quietly sitting in the presence of God, trusting Him to give us what we need for each day. We live in a constantly moving, noisy world. For many of us, being quiet may be the hardest discipline to make a daily habit. This week, ask God to give you eyes to see and ears to hear the importance of this discipline. And if you're already in a good rhythm with quiet, stillness, and listening ~ ask God to show you what more He has for you and how to take the next steps.

—————————————— PSALM 46 ——————————————

For the director of music. Of the Sons of Korah. According to alamoth. A song.

[1] God is our refuge and strength, an ever-present help in trouble. [2] Therefore we will not fear, though the earth give way and the mountains fall into the heart of the sea, [3] though its waters roar and foam and the mountains quake with their surging.

[4] There is a river whose streams make glad the city of God, the holy place where the Most High dwells. [5] God is within her, she will not fall; God will help her at break of day. [6] Nations are in uproar, kingdoms fall; he lifts his voice, the earth melts. [7] The Lord Almighty is with us; the God of Jacob is our fortress. [8] Come and see what the Lord has done, the desolations he has brought on the earth. [9] He makes wars cease to the ends of the earth. He breaks the bow and shatters the spear; he burns the shields with fire. [10] He says, "Be still, and know that I am God; I will be exalted among the nations, I will be exalted in the earth." [11] The Lord Almighty is with us; the God of Jacob is our fortress.

SESSION QUESTIONS

—

WEEK TWO

DAY 01

What's on your agenda for the day? Likely, you have a list of things to accomplish that will carry you from the moment you wake to the moment you crash into bed tonight. What about the command we just read in Psalm 46 to " be still and know that I am God", to talk with Him and then take time to listen? Is that part of the plan? Read through the following passages: Psalm 46:10-11, Psalm 62:5-8, Isaiah 30:18, Isaiah 40:31, Lamentations 3:22-26. Choose one passage to read a few times over and pray through as you come before God. After you've spent a few minutes talking to God, take 5 minutes to listen. Shut everything out, fight for silence and space to listen and receive!

DAY 02

Have you heard Jesus speak to you? Maybe you're not sure if you have ever truly heard Him speak. Read John 10:1-18 and write down what Jesus says is true of those who have put their trust in Him. Most often, God speaks through His Word, through other believers, and often times we just know in our hearts during times of prayer or worship that He has spoken something specific to us. What God says will always align with His Word. Today as you pray, take 5 minutes to sit in silence and ask Jesus to speak to you and to give you ears to hear.

DAY 03

Are you a "doer?" Do people lean on you to plan and execute? Where does "being" with Jesus fit into that picture? Read through the story of Mary and Martha in Luke 10:38-42 with fresh eyes. What do you see? Take special note of Jesus' perspective of the "one thing needed." Write out a prayer to God in response to this "one thing." Continue in your quest to be quiet and allow your heart to hear from Jesus. Create time again today to open your hands and heart to receive.

DAY 04

Read Mark 1:35, Luke 5:16 and Matthew 6:6 from the Message version and the NIV. The Gospels record many times where Jesus took time to withdraw and be alone with the Father. Our Savior made it a priority to get away to pray and receive. He knew that to fulfill His purpose here, He needed time to talk with God and hear from Him. What is God revealing to you about His desire for you to come to Him? End your time in prayer with space for stillness and silence in His presence. Write down any Scripture, conviction, or expression of love He speaks to you.

DAY 05

There is great value in creating daily time to simply BE with Jesus. Keep working to minimize distractions and have consistent time to sit at His feet to listen and receive. This is a battle so worth fighting! When we draw near to Him, He will draw near to us! (James 4:8.) What Scripture impacted your heart most this week? Wrap up the week with prayer and a time of quiet. Be sure to reflect in your journal how this week has impacted your daily time with Jesus.

Finish the week by reading 1 Thessalonians 2:1-12.

WHOLE & HOLY

GO FAST TO FIND FREEDOM

—

Fasting. It's amazing how just a day without something we love and rely upon can bring out some hidden attitudes and reactions that we didn't even know were there. What is fasting? It's voluntarily going without food, a habit, or material item in order to focus on prayer and relationship with God. As we fast, we begin to see how dependent we've become on things other than Jesus to help us keep our cool, to have peace, and satisfaction. Fasting creates the opportunity to lean into the heart of the Father and to pray more fervently for Him alone to consume us and fill all our needs. We need Jesus more than we need anything else. Posturing our lives regularly to do without in order to draw nearer to Him is always a win. Fasting does require that we give something up for a time, but in the end, what we can gain is far greater than anything we'll ever give up.

[1] Jesus, full of the Holy Spirit, left the Jordan and was led by the Spirit into the wilderness, [2] where for forty days he was tempted by the devil. He ate nothing during those days, and at the end of them he was hungry. [3] The devil said to him, "If you are the Son of God, tell this stone to become bread." [4] Jesus answered, "It is written: 'Man shall not live on bread alone.'" [5] The devil led him up to a high place and showed him in an instant all the kingdoms of the world. [6] And he said to him, "I will give you all their authority and splendor; it has been given to me, and I can give it to anyone I want to. [7] If you worship me, it will all be yours." [8] Jesus answered, "It is written: 'Worship the Lord your God and serve him only.'" [9] The devil led him to Jerusalem and had him stand on the highest point of the temple. "If you are the Son of God," he said, "throw yourself down from here. [10] For it is written: "'He will command his angels concerning you to guard you carefully; [11] they will lift you up in their hands, so that you will not strike your foot against a stone.'" [12] Jesus answered, "It is said: 'Do not put the Lord your God to the test.'" [13] When the devil had finished all this tempting, he left him until an opportune time.

SESSION QUESTIONS

—

WEEK THREE

DAY 01 Doing without. That's not typically a choice we'd move toward first. Everywhere we turn today there's a reminder to "get," take care of yourself, satisfy your need, do what you want. In God's economy, however, we're called to live with a very different attitude; one that says deny self, take up your cross, serve others. Today, read Luke 4:1-13 and meditate on this passage in preparation for tomorrow. Also, journal your understanding of what it means to fast and how that's incorporated, or not, into your life.

DAY 02 Read Jesus' account in the wilderness in Luke 4:1-13 again. What was the purpose of Jesus fasting during those 40 days and nights? What was the result? What does Jesus demonstrate for us in this passage of Scripture?

DAY 03 Fasting causes us to pull back from the normal rhythms of life. When we deny ourselves an earthly comfort, we often find that there are things we may be more devoted to than our relationship with Jesus. Fasting reveals. It helps you put your physical nature in its place so your spirit can draw closer to Him. Read Psalm 24:1-6 and Psalm 51:10 and write out anything that you see as an idol in your life whether food, drink, media, a hobby, or another person.

DAY 04 When we fast, the motive is never about trying to get God to do something for us. It is always about submitting ourselves to Him with a willingness to be changed and to better align our lives with His. When we remove things we've become dependent on that are not of Him, it allows Jesus to become our focus, central in all we do. Read Isaiah 58 to gain more perspective on what God desires when we fast and record any revelations you receive.

DAY 05 Take time today to pray and listen. Ask God if there is something you need to fast from. It could be a commitment one day a week fasting from food, or taking a couple of weeks to fast from a particular food or drink. How prominent is social media in your life? Maybe it's time to take a break! Talk to God about it first, then share with your mentor, a close friend, or another mentee and invite them to walk with you in this.

Continue practicing these habits and routines as we head into weeks 4-8.
End the week by reading 1 Thessalonians 2:13-20

WHOLE & HOLY

WORDS MATTER

—

SPIRIT, **SOUL** & BODY

As a reminder, the Holy Spirit leads our spirit, our spirit leads our soul, and our soul leads our body. Your soul houses your will, intellect, emotion, but don't be confused. Your mind and your brain are not the same. Your brain is a part of your physical body which takes its cues from your soul and your mind-which are one and the same! We don't want to get overly technical, but we do need to understand that your soul, and the influences on it, directly impact your overall well-being mentally, emotionally, and physically. In Psalm 119 King David declared "I have hidden your Word in my heart that I might not sin against You." He understood that what we hide deep in our hearts, impacts our beliefs, which impacts our thoughts and the decisions we make. So what lies unseen within you inspires how you live. With that in mind, let's look at what the Word says about your mind!

The words we speak, hear, and dwell on influence and shape who we are. Most of the time, the thoughts that impact us the most are the ones that silently play in our own minds, that internal dialogue that goes on throughout the day. Think about what the conversation in your head sounds like and where it comes from. Maybe the dialogue finds its root in beliefs you've adopted throughout life. Sometimes the words are good. Sometimes, not so good. And it's probably peppered with pronouncements others have spoken over you. Even when the words hurt and you desperately don't want to believe them, somehow those can stick in your soul and take on a power that is hard to identify and even harder to control. For Jesus-followers, the good news is that we're not powerless. We can allow the loudest voice in our hearts and minds to encourage, build up, strengthen, and bring wisdom – not tear down. So for that, we have to first identify anything that is not from Jesus and then replace it with truth that brings life.

PHILIPPIANS 4:8-9

[8] Finally, brothers and sisters, whatever is true, whatever is noble, whatever is right, whatever is pure, whatever is lovely, whatever is admirable—if anything is excellent or praiseworthy—think about such things. [9] Whatever you have learned or received or heard from me, or seen in me—put it into practice. And the God of peace will be with you.

SESSION QUESTIONS

—

WEEK FOUR

DAY 01   Start the week reading Phil 4:8-9. Take time today to really think on and pray through this passage. As you walk through your day, make note of your thoughts and what influences how you speak and the decisions you make. Would you say your thoughts are led by whatever is true, noble, right, pure, lovely, etc.? Begin to journal anything that doesn't line up with this Scripture. Naming it will help you change it.

DAY 02   Satan loves to throw lies our way to discourage us and distract us from the truth. It's important to come to terms with this reality right up front in our study. Our minds are a target for the enemy! Read John 8:44. Ask the Holy Spirit to continue to show you any lies and negative influences that you've chosen to believe that are not from Jesus. Continue to write them out. We'll be coming back to them later in the study.

DAY 03   After taking time the last couple of days to evaluate your thoughts, what has surprised you most? With those revelations before you, read the following Scriptures: 1 Corinthians 2:14-16, John 15:14-15 and 2 Timothy 1:6-7 KJV. What do these passages reveal about your mind? How does that land on your heart?

DAY 04   It is easy to grab hold of wrong ideas and process thoughts in a way that pollute our heart and soul. At times, we do this unknowingly. Other times it's a result of leaving ourselves wide open and exposed to whatever comes our way. Read Proverbs 4:23-27 and Luke 6:45. Take time to sit in these passages today. How can you be vigilant in guarding your heart?

DAY 05   Before we head into next week, work on memorizing Philippians 4:8-9. It is the perfect foundation for where we're headed next! Be diligent about your mind and guard against beliefs and thoughts that pop up that you know do not line up with truth. Write these down as they come to you so that you'll be more aware of the deceptive tactics of Satan.

End the week by reading 1 Thessalonians 3

DECLARATIONS OF TRUTH

—

Lies and negative thoughts are sneaky. They find a way into our heart and soul and take up residence before we're even aware of their presence. Sometimes we can immediately determine where they came from. Other lies are not so easy to identify, and can be the fruit of things buried deep in our hearts from years past. In 2 Corinthians 10:3-6 we're reminded that the world is unprincipled and doesn't fight fair. Thankfully, we don't fight our battles the way the world does. We've been given everything we need to stand firm against any spiritual ambush. Through the power of the Spirit, we can take every thought to Jesus and begin to shape it and change it to reflect His heart! How? As we engage our minds and apply the Word of God, truth takes root, grows, and saturates our lives. As it thrives, it becomes the prevailing voice that we hear and ultimately, alters the way we live. This week, you'll be challenged to take up the Word of God, to demolish lies and false beliefs, and become more deeply establish in the truth.

—————————— JOHN 8:31-32 ——————————

[31] To the Jews who had believed him, Jesus said, "If you hold to my teaching, you are really my disciples. [32] Then you will know the truth, and the truth will set you free."

SESSION QUESTIONS

—

WEEK FIVE

DAY 01
The Word of God has many amazing promises that can change your life. When you consistently speak, pray, and worship through the Word, you can be certain that there will be a beautiful return! Read these passages of Scripture and underline every reference to God's Word and the promises connected to them: Isaiah 55:8-13, Hebrews 4:12, Psalm 19:7-11 and John 8:31-32. This week, look back at the list of false beliefs and lies that you made from week 4 and choose one that you battle often. Find a verse that quiets that lie and re-establishes the truth. Write it down. Begin to declare that truth over that lie daily and whenever it shows up in your thoughts. For example: LIE: I've gone too far or sinned too much for God to truly love me. TRUTH: Through Jesus I have forgiveness from all sin and I'm free from shame and condemnation. Nothing can keep me from the love of God. 1 John 1:9, Romans 8:1-2, 38-39.

DAY 02
Read Romans 12:2, Psalm 42 and 43. Beliefs can run deep, but as we read yesterday, the Word cuts to the deepest part of who we are and brings change ~ Hebrews 4:12! If you're feeling the weight of lies, know that your mind can be renewed. Take note of King David's actions in Psalm 42-43. Journal what Jesus reveals to you in these Scriptures. Add to your list of declarations. Example: If worry, fear, and anxiety are your close companions because of lies, declare these truths: I will trust in the Lord with all my heart, and choose to turn my worries into prayers. I can cast all my care on Jesus and trust Him to bring peace to my heart. He cares for me! 1 Peter 5:7, Proverbs 3:5-6, Philippians 4:6-7.

DAY 03
Read Ephesians 6:10-17 today along with 1 Peter 5:8-9. What stands out to you in both these passages? How did Jesus battle the lies and temptations of Satan while in the wilderness (week 3, Luke 4:1-13). How does verse 17 of Ephesians 6 describe God's Word? Take time to write out a new declaration today. If you need help finding a Scripture, reach out to your mentor.

As we saw yesterday, Jesus beautifully leads the way in showing us how to employ the Word of God as a weapon. Continue to fight for freedom from lies and for truth to reign in your life through the renewing of your mind. Read James 1:2-8. What stands out to you in this passage that applies to this battle? Keep building your list of declarations.

We have thoughts, images, and voices coming at us from many different directions. Some that we can't change or control. What we do have the power to do is continually guard our heart and soul with truth! A strong soul, full of godly wisdom, will lead us to make wise choices regarding our purity, physical health, and how we choose to use our lives for God's service. Add to your list of declarations again today and finish up by reading Colossians 2:6-7 and Psalm 19:14. Share some final thoughts on this week.

Continue declaring truth daily to shut down false beliefs. It can take some time but as you commit to this daily, truth will become more deeply rooted and lead to freedom.

End this week with 1 Thessalonians 4:1-12

WHOLE & HOLY

THE VALUE OF YOU

—

SPIRIT, SOUL & **BODY**

We've focused on how to pursue health and wholeness in our relationship with Jesus and in our thought life, and now we're diving into what it means to be healthy, whole, and holy when it comes to our bodies. Your physical health is as important as your spiritual and emotional health. Think about it. How often has a headache, bad cold or other physical ailment affected your emotions? Have you ever snapped at the ones you love when you are tired and run down? Are you less prone to read the Word and pray when you don't feel very good? Our overall physical health impacts the way we think, feel and process everything and it impacts the way we interact with the people around us. As a believer, your body is a temple of the Holy Spirit. God has taken up residence in you. Your body houses your spirit and soul, so pursuing physical vitality matters and honors God deeply. For the last portion of this session, we'll be reminded that as His temple, we are privileged to glorify Him by protecting, nourishing, and strengthening ourselves.

——

You are an amazing creation! A beautiful masterpiece! Perfectly planned and molded by the Creator of the Universe! Not only that, having put your faith and trust in Jesus Christ, the Holy Spirit actually resides in you. That is a massive truth to wrap our hearts around! Many of us might find it somewhat challenging to truthfully say that our daily thoughts about ourselves reflect this truth. We are meant to carry His Name to the nations. Our lives are now poised to reflect the beauty of the Father to the world. But so often, how we care for, carry, and see ourselves is quite the opposite of the esteemed position that's been given by God. Open your heart this week to truly receive Jesus' love and begin to embrace the value He places on your life.

———— 1 CORINTHIANS 6:19-20 ————

[19] Do you not know that your bodies are temples of the Holy Spirit, who is in you, whom you have received from God? You are not your own; [20] you were bought at a price. Therefore honor God with your bodies.

SESSION QUESTIONS

—

WEEK SIX

DAY 01

So, let's have some real talk. What value do you place on who you are? How do you see yourself? Take a few minutes and honestly write out your thoughts and feelings about you. Read Genesis 1:26-31, 1 Corinthians 6:19-20, and Psalm 45:10-12 (from the Message Paraphrase) and then reflect on anything new Jesus reveals to you about the value and beauty He places on your life.

DAY 02

Look again at 1 Corinthians 6:19-20. How does this verse land on your heart personally to hear "you are not your own, you've been bought with a price?" Be completely honest. Do you find it easy to bring your whole heart and every expression of who you are under the reign of Jesus? Are there areas of your life that you'd rather not surrender to Him? Write out your response to these questions in your journal. Your truthful answers may be the starting point that will help you face some deep issues that you have tried to keep hidden from yourself.

DAY 03

Read Psalm 139:13-18. This is a passage that may feel very familiar to many. Ask God to give you fresh eyes to see something new today! Have you ever tried any kind of needle craft or do you know someone who does it well? Think about the intricacies of knitting and how the hands of God "knit" you together. Take some time to do a word study on the Hebrew meaning of the words fearfully and wonderfully. Would you say your everyday life choices reflect those truths? Write your thoughts in your journal.

DAY 04

Jesus created you and has given you a beautiful life to live. You are a temple of the Holy Spirit. He is in you! So let's talk purity from the inside out. If you really embrace the reality of the Holy Spirit's presence in your life, would it change how you protect your purity and as a result, inform the way you talk, dress, live? Does how you live line up with the true value of who you are in Jesus? Write out a prayer to God in response to these questions today.

DAY 05

Wrap up this week by memorizing Zephaniah 3:17. You are loved with a love that is pure, powerful, and life changing. Walk in that love and the knowledge of whose you are and who you are! Let your life reflect that to the world around you!

End your time today reading 1 Thessalonians 4:13-18

WHOLE & HOLY

NOURISH

—

As we read in Scripture last week, you are a temple of the Holy Spirit. That truth should translate into how you think about and care for yourself, resulting in a desire to thoughtfully nourish what you've been given. But let's be real. Gentle attention for bodies isn't always what we do, is it? We either find ourselves over indulging our desires by eating and drinking whatever we please (often, to excess). Or we can become obsessed with eating healthy and unintentionally become slaves to our bodies in a different way. If we're not careful, we can end up creating idols out of food and health. Food is a gift from God. We're told to receive it as grace and honor God in everything we do. So, this week we'll work toward bringing this area of our lives under the Lordship of Jesus to find peace, strength, self-discipline, and holiness. Take time to listen and let the Holy Spirit lead and teach you how to receive this gift of grace so that you can make wise choices to care for the life you've been given.

—————————— 1 CORINTHIANS 10:31 ——————————

[31] So whether you eat or drink or whatever you do, do it all for the glory of God.

SESSION QUESTIONS

WEEK SEVEN

DAY 01   When we have a clear understanding of truth and who we are in Christ, the overflow is a desire to honor Him through our daily (and even mundane) choices. What we put into our bodies is yet another expression of how we value ourselves. Those decisions which directly correlate to health, strength and vitality will impact us either positively or negatively. Read 1 Corinthians 10:31. Simply sit in that commandment and think about how you nourish your body. Journal your thoughts.

DAY 02   You've been bought, redeemed, set free. But in your new position in Christ, God allows us a free will to make choices. Truth is, we all sometimes choose to consume food and drinks that are not the best. But set aside those infrequent indulgences and think specifically about your regular habits. Read 1 Corinthians 10:23-24. Is there anything you eat or drink that you feel convicted about? Write down anything that comes to mind and bring that before God in prayer.

DAY 03   There is no space for our affections to be divided. Though we might agree that Jesus needs first place in our lives, oftentimes, without realizing it, we can turn to food for satisfaction and contentment, instead of Him. Read Proverbs 23:19-21, Romans 13:14, Galatians 6:7-9, 1 Corinthians 10:13. Reflect on what stands out to you or resonates with your heart. Honestly wrestle with how your affections may or may not be divided.

DAY 04   God created us with an appetite. And He wants us to enjoy food and even feasting on occasion. Food is not an enemy. It is given by God for your good, and meant to nourish, strengthen, heal, and satisfy. But through self-discipline and wisdom, it's up to us to make choices to feed our body well. Regardless of where you are in that pursuit, stay the course! If you're not eating enough, or eating too much, or simply consuming foods that bring harm and not health, it all needs to be brought under the rule of Jesus in our lives. Read Hebrews 12:1, Galatians 5:22-23, 2 Peter 1:3-8, and revisit Galatians 6:7-9 from yesterday. Write out a prayer to God in response to these truths today.

We have this one life, one body. God has given us all we need to have wisdom and self-control to take care of ourselves. We honor Jesus by how we honor our bodies as a temple of the Holy Spirit! Read Matthew 22:34-40 to wrap up this week. Record in your journal the main truths that impacted your heart the most this week.

End your time today reading 1 Thessalonians 5:1-15

WHOLE & HOLY

STRENGTH IS FOR SERVICE

—

In this final week, we're leaning into the truth that we're called to serve and be a part of the bigger story God is writing in and through us as His Church. How beautiful to be included in God's work here in this life! We trust Jesus to be our ultimate strength giver, provider, and the One who will do it. But it's our responsibility to daily choose to take up our honored position, and to love Him with all our heart, soul, mind and strength. We bring the very best we have as a response of worship to His amazing love and goodness toward us! He's given us life, now we get to steward it and live for His name and renown.

ROMANS 15:1-6

[1] We who are strong ought to bear with the failings of the weak and not to please ourselves. [2] Each of us should please our neighbors for their good, to build them up. [3] For even Christ did not please himself but, as it is written: "The insults of those who insult you have fallen on me." [4] For everything that was written in the past was written to teach us, so that through the endurance taught in the Scriptures and the encouragement they provide we might have hope. [5] May the God who gives endurance and encouragement give you the same attitude of mind toward each other that Christ Jesus had, [6] so that with one mind and one voice you may glorify the God and Father of our Lord Jesus Christ.

SESSION QUESTIONS

———

WEEK EIGHT

DAY 01   Being whole and holy in our bodies is more than reaching health goals to live longer and feel better. It allows us greater opportunity to serve the Lord and bring Him glory. When we care for ourselves, we can better carry what God gives us and then, in turn, extend loving concern for others in our world. This pursuit is unique and specific to each of us individually! Let's jump right in. Read Romans 15:1-6 in the NIV and The Message version. Are you using your life and strength for the good of others? How so? If not, you can begin right now. Ask God to show you where you can go or what you can do to serve Him by serving others.

DAY 02   Read Romans 15:2 in the Message again today. Reflect on the truth that "strength is for service not status." If your life is being leveraged for the good of others, take an honest look at your motives. Do they line up with this truth?

DAY 03   We've exercised and challenged our spirit and soul over the past 7 weeks. Our body, likewise, needs to be exercised physically for health and strength. Read 1 Timothy 4:8 and 1 Corinthians 9:26-27. Is physical exercise a part of your weekly routine? Take time to consider the benefits of exercising and how you can begin to incorporate this into a healthier lifestyle.

DAY 04   Read Proverbs 31:17, 1 Peter 4:10-11 and Proverbs 11:24-25. Think about how these Scriptures line up with the idea of strength is for service. Jot down any of the benefits of being physically healthy as they relate specifically to serving Jesus.

DAY 05   Because of who Jesus is and what He's done for us, we want our lives to count for His name and renown (Ps 135:13). As everyday opportunities to love and serve others present themselves, we want our response to be like that of Jesus. Read 1 Peter 2:9, Philippians 2:1-4, Matthew 20:26-28, and Mark 8:34-35. Reflect on these passages under the theme of "strength for service" and write out whatever Jesus brings to light. Are you currently plugged in at your Church to serve? How might you give more of yourself so that others could encounter Jesus?

Finish your time today and this session by reading 1 Thessalonians 5:16-28

UNDER NEW MANAGEMENT

SESSION THREE

Have you ever seen a sign hanging in the window of a favorite business that read "Under New Management"? You may not know anything about what took place in a board room or in a lawyer's office that lead to posting the sign, but a banner like this does tell you one thing: Things have changed. Under the direction of the new owners, people who stop by can expect to experience a new way of doing business. It might mean new methods, new purpose, new goals, new procedures and maybe even complete renovation and a whole new look. And the point of it all is to improve the effectiveness and operation of the company. In simplified terms that is a lot like what happened to you when you gave your life to Jesus. Psalm 24:1-2

reminds us of who owns this world with the bold declaration: "The earth is the Lord's and everything in it, the world, and all who live in it!" First Corinthians 6:20 goes on to tell every believer that through the sacrifice of Jesus, you have been "bought with a price." In economic terms, that means that once you become a follower of Jesus, He holds the title deed to your life. As "new owner" He has the right to make necessary changes in methods, function and appearance, and even do a whole renovation, so that everything about you now reflects His purpose and goals. In this session we'll dive into the life of Jesus as recorded in the Gospel of Mark. As we discover more of who He is, and understand His power and authority, we will continue to relinquish our position as 'owner' and take up the humble and grateful attitude of servant and steward of all that He has placed in our hands.

THE GOSPEL OF MARK

Jesus. Just say His name in a group of strangers and you can expect to get some kind of reaction. It might be an affirming smile from others who know Him as Savior and friend. But it might just as easily be an enraged look of anger from those who oppose Him. Or even a dismissive sigh of indifference from skeptics and doubters. However, in the wide range of possible responses, chances are they have at least heard something about the man called Jesus. A few thousand years ago, that would not be the case. Most of those living in the days of the Gospel writers didn't know much, if anything, about the man who confidently called Himself the Son of God. If you can put yourself in their place for a minute, imagine what you might have thought if you'd heard rumors about a relatively unknown man who showed up and said the things that Jesus said. Of course, there was confusion and much skepticism. But the miracles He performed and the authority that Jesus taught were, well, undeniable. How could you argue with Bartimaeus, who was blind for so many years but was later walking around the town with perfect vision? (Mk. 10:46-52) Or with Jairus, whose daughter once was confirmed to be dead, but was raised to life and given back to him? (Mk. 5:22-43) Or with the thousands of people who actually ate and were satisfied from a couple of fish and few loaves of bread? (Mk. 6:30-44; 8:1-13) And that's just the beginning of what Jesus accomplished on Earth. The record of what actually happened to real people in real places forms the basis of Mark's Gospel. Under the inspiration of the Holy Spirit, he set out to write down the events so that the people who hadn't met Jesus firsthand could understand and also believe. While this writer of the second and shortest Gospel wasn't one of the twelve disciples of Christ during His life on earth, John Mark (or simply, Mark) was part of the early church and is mentioned in the books of Acts, Colossians, Philippians, and Second Timothy. For a time he was an associate of Paul, but their sometimes difficult relationship caused them to part ways for a while before eventually reconciling their differences near the end of Paul's life. So, if Mark didn't know Jesus personally nor did he follow Paul, where did his information come from? And how can we know that it's reliable? History suggests that most of the information for the writing of this letter to the Gentile converts in the city of Rome came from his relationship with a very reliable source: Peter.

In 55-59 AD, (estimated time of authorship of Mark's Gospel) Christianity was in its infancy, consisting of a relatively small number of scattered followers. There were no written records of the life of Jesus (Mark's Gospel was penned first) and very few people outside Jerusalem knew much about the Rabbi who lived, taught and was eventually executed in that area of Palestine. So, guided by the Spirit of God, Mark addressed his letter to those outside the Jewish faith in order to affirm Christ's identity. His words continue to challenge each of us today to come face-to-face with Jesus… fully man, fully God, who lived, died and was resurrected and is now seated on the throne in heaven. So as we dive into Mark's Gospel, set aside your skepticism, cultural traditions, or preconceived ideas, and just meet Jesus.

SESSION GOALS

UNDER NEW MANAGEMENT

GOALS

- To identify Jesus as Ruler of all and acknowledge His right to direct our lives
- To bring our lives in line with the teachings of Scripture in order to foster spiritual growth and development
- To loosen our dependence on possessions, habits, attitudes and/or relationships that block our devotion to Jesus.
- To help us see her ordinary tasks as usable by God for extraordinary purposes.
- To apply the mindset and mission of Jesus to all aspects of our lives.

QUESTIONS

- What's the difference between an owner and a manager? Apply that to your relationship to Jesus.
- Describe any changes that have been made in your life since you became under the new management of Jesus? What other changes need to be made?
- What area of your life (time, money, relationships, etc.) is the most difficult to turn over to Jesus? Why do you think this is the case?
- Sometimes it's hard to relate the events of Jesus' life to life right now. What challenge for living today do you take away from the Gospel of Mark?

UNDER NEW MANAGEMENT

THE NEW OWNER

MARK 1:1-20

[1] The beginning of the good news about Jesus the Messiah, the Son of God, [2] as it is written in Isaiah the prophet: "I will send my messenger ahead of you, who will prepare your way" — [3] "a voice of one calling in the wilderness, 'Prepare the way for the Lord, make straight paths for him.'" [4] And so John the Baptist appeared in the wilderness, preaching a baptism of repentance for the forgiveness of sins. [5] The whole Judean countryside and all the people of Jerusalem went out to him. Confessing their sins, they were baptized by him in the Jordan River. [6] John wore clothing made of camel's hair, with a leather belt around his waist, and he ate locusts and wild honey. [7] And this was his message: "After me comes the one more powerful than I, the straps of whose sandals I am not worthy to stoop down and untie. [8] I baptize you with water, but he will baptize you with the Holy Spirit." [9] At that time Jesus came from Nazareth in Galilee and was baptized by John in the Jordan. [10] Just as Jesus was coming up out of the water, he saw heaven being torn open and the Spirit descending on him like a dove. [11] And a voice came from heaven: "You are my Son, whom I love; with you I am well pleased." [12] At once the Spirit sent him out into the wilderness, [13] and he was in the wilderness forty days, being tempted by Satan. He was with the wild animals, and angels attended him. [14] After John was put in prison, Jesus went into Galilee, proclaiming the good news of God. [15] "The time has come," he said. "The kingdom of God has come near. Repent and believe the good news!" [16] As Jesus walked beside the Sea of Galilee, he saw Simon and his brother Andrew casting a net into the lake, for they were fishermen. [17] "Come, follow me," Jesus said, "and I will send you out to fish for people." [18] At once they left their nets and followed him. [19] When he had gone a little farther, he saw James son of Zebedee and his brother John in a boat, preparing their nets. [20] Without delay he called them, and they left their father Zebedee in the boat with the hired men and followed him.

SESSION QUESTIONS

—

WEEK ONE

DAY 01 Hollywood movies often begin with a high impact action sequence to capture your attention. Notice the high level of action surrounding the authority of Jesus in the first chapter of this Gospel. Underline anything that captures your attention.

DAY 02 Mark introduces us to Jesus differently than any of the other Gospel writers. He writes nothing about Christ's background or history, but instead gives us His credentials. Look at the first 11 verses to find 3 individuals/groups who give witness and approval to Christ. Why are these important to us?

DAY 03 Read through Mark 1:12-13, 21-28 (cross reference Matt. 4:1-11) to get a better understanding of Christ's authority over the spirit world. Also, look up Rom. 8:38-39; Phil 2:9-11. What do you learn about Christ's superiority? Write in your journal how this can provide stability to your world.

DAY 04 Read back over Mark 1:29-45. Why do you think verse 35 is included in the middle of this section? What's its relevance to the rest of the passage and entire chapter? Relate it to your busy and demanding work and home life.

DAY 05 End this week by reading all of Mark 1 & 2. Note specifically the response of Simon, James, John & Levi to the call of Jesus. (see also, Luke 5:1-11; and for other responses to the Lord, see Isaiah 6:1-8; Phil 3:7-9) Think about what you learned about Jesus' authority this week. What it would take for you to have a "leave everything" moment? Remember that could include relationships, dreams, desires, interests as well as physical locations. Journal your thoughts.

UNDER NEW MANAGEMENT

CULTIVATING SPIRITUAL GROWTH

———

MARK 4:1-20

[1] Again Jesus began to teach by the lake. The crowd that gathered around him was so large that he got into a boat and sat in it out on the lake, while all the people were along the shore at the water's edge. [2] He taught them many things by parables, and in his teaching said: [3] "Listen! A farmer went out to sow his seed. [4] As he was scattering the seed, some fell along the path, and the birds came and ate it up. [5] Some fell on rocky places, where it did not have much soil. It sprang up quickly, because the soil was shallow. [6] But when the sun came up, the plants were scorched, and they withered because they had no root. [7] Other seed fell among thorns, which grew up and choked the plants, so that they did not bear grain. [8] Still other seed fell on good soil. It came up, grew and produced a crop, some multiplying thirty, some sixty, some a hundred times."

[9] Then Jesus said, "Whoever has ears to hear, let them hear." [10] When he was alone, the Twelve and the others around

him asked him about the parables. [11] He told them, "The secret of the kingdom of God has been given to you. But to those on the outside everything is said in parables [12] so that,"'they may be ever seeing but never perceiving, and ever hearing but never understanding; otherwise they might turn and be forgiven!'"

[13] Then Jesus said to them, "Don't you understand this parable? How then will you understand any parable? [14] The farmer sows the word. [15] Some people are like seed along the path, where the word is sown. As soon as they hear it, Satan comes and takes away the word that was sown in them. [16] Others, like seed sown on rocky places, hear the word and at once receive it with joy. [17] But since they have no root, they last only a short time. When trouble or persecution comes because of the word, they quickly fall away. [18] Still others, like seed sown among thorns, hear the word; [19] but the worries of this life, the deceitfulness of wealth and the desires for other things come in and choke the word, making it unfruitful. [20] Others, like seed sown on good soil, hear the word, accept it, and produce a crop—some thirty, some sixty, some a hundred times what was sown."

SESSION QUESTIONS

—

WEEK TWO

01
Read all of Mark 3 & 4 in one sitting. How do the verses for this week fit into the other things Mark says in these chapters? Can you see a common theme emerge? Usually the Gospels don't contain a direct explanation of the parables by Jesus Himself. Why do you think one is included for this one?

02
Often the Parable of the Sower is taught as a lesson about salvation, but it can also be applied to believers as well. Consider the four types of ground that the good seed fell on. Identify times when you exhibited all four of these types of soil. What made the difference in what your life yielded? Be sure to think about how certain environments, activities or people influence your response to the truth.

03
Ever had "one of those days?" How about a nagging physical pain that just won't go away? Or a co-worker/roommate/family member who keeps getting on your nerves? Read verses 4-6 & 15-17. Think about how a bad mood, a preexisting opinion, difficulties, etc. cause your heart to become un-productive like hardened dirt of "the path" or lead to immature growth like seed in the rocky soil? Jot down a brief prayer that could be used to invite the Spirit of God to soften the soil of your heart during times when your interest in spiritual growth is low.

04
What's bothering you today? Any worries with the family? Anxiety about the future? Some big decision that needs to be made soon? With those things in mind, think about the third type of soil in verses 7 & 18-19. How do daily concerns distract you from the things of God? Write in your journal what the following verses say about worry and anxiety: Ps 56:3-4; Matt. 6:25-34; Phil 4:6-7; Heb. 13:5-6; 1 Peter 5:6-7. What can you change today that would fertilize your life to become the good soil that yields fruit?

05
Mark 4:21-34 gives three shorter parables. Do you think they might be teaching a similar lesson about faith in God? Read through verse 35-41 to see how Jesus tested the disciples' understanding of the parables. Did they grasp what He taught? Why or why not? How has God tested your understanding of spiritual truth in the past? What was the result?

UNDER NEW MANAGEMENT

MANAGING DESPERATION

—

MARK 5:21-43

²¹ When Jesus had again crossed over by boat to the other side of the lake, a large crowd gathered around him while he was by the lake. ²² Then one of the synagogue leaders, named Jairus, came, and when he saw Jesus, he fell at his feet. ²³ He pleaded earnestly with him, "My little daughter is dying. Please come and put your hands on her so that she will be healed and live." ²⁴ So Jesus went with him. A large crowd followed and pressed around him. ²⁵ And a woman was there who had been subject to bleeding for twelve years. ²⁶ She had suffered a great deal under the care of many doctors and had spent all she had, yet instead of getting better she grew worse. ²⁷ When she heard about Jesus, she came up behind him in the crowd and touched his cloak, ²⁸ because she thought, "If I just touch his clothes, I will be healed." ²⁹ Immediately her bleeding stopped and she felt in her body that she was freed from her suffering. ³⁰ At once Jesus realized that power had gone out from him. He turned around in the crowd and asked, "Who touched my clothes?" ³¹ "You see the people crowding against you," his disciples answered, "and yet you can ask, 'Who touched me?'" ³² But Jesus kept looking around to see who had done it. ³³ Then the woman, knowing what had happened to her, came and fell at his feet and, trembling with fear, told him the whole truth. ³⁴ He said to her, "Daughter, your faith has healed you. Go in peace and be freed from your suffering."

³⁵ While Jesus was still speaking, some people came from the house of Jairus, the synagogue leader. "Your daughter is dead," they said. "Why bother the teacher anymore?" ³⁶ Overhearing what they said, Jesus told him, "Don't be afraid; just believe."

³⁷ He did not let anyone follow him except Peter, James and John the brother of James. ³⁸ When they came to the home of the synagogue leader, Jesus saw a commotion, with people crying and wailing loudly. ³⁹ He went in and said to them, "Why all this commotion and wailing? The child is not dead but asleep." ⁴⁰ But they laughed at him.

After he put them all out, he took the child's father and mother and the disciples who were with him, and went in where the child was. ⁴¹ He took her by the hand and said to her, "Talitha koum!" (which means "Little girl, I say to you, get up!"). ⁴² Immediately the girl stood up and began to walk around (she was twelve years old). At this they were completely astonished. ⁴³ He gave strict orders not to let anyone know about this, and told them to give her something to eat.

SESSION QUESTIONS

—

DAY 01 Start this week's study by reading Mark 5, paying attention to the faith of the three people who received miracles from Jesus. What is their attitude before the miracle? What happened as a result? From this, what can you conclude is the purpose for any miracle, both then and now?

DAY 02 Look back through the verses about the woman who touched Jesus from the crowd (vs 24-34). Relate any physical problems you may have to what she might have endured. How do these types of desperate situations cross over from the physical to also affect your whole being, mentally, spiritually, emotionally, financially, etc?

DAY 03 Reread verse 21-34. This is the only instance recorded in which Jesus referred to any woman as "daughter." In doing so, He gave her what she wanted (healing) and what she never expected (relationship). Remember that through faith in Jesus, you are also "daughter" to God (Gal. 4:4-7). How could embracing that designation change your attitude about your problems even if they never change on this earth? Write down what you see in Eph. 3:14-21 about the depth of love that is yours in Christ.

DAY 04 Move on to Mark 6. What do you learn about the importance of faith from each of the stories recorded in this chapter?

DAY 05 Go over verses 45-56 again. Then read the parallel passage in Matt 14:22-33. Have you ever felt like you were "straining at the oars because the wind was against you?" Take some time to honestly tell God about your frustration, disappointment and anguish. Journal your genuine emotions as you, like Peter, call out to Jesus to save you, trusting that He will steady you even if the storm rages on. Close your time today with gratitude.

**It can sometimes take a significant amount of time to deal with deep emotion that stems from hurt, loss and disappointment. If necessary, continue to wrestle with these ideas with the goal of yielding them to Jesus as the session moves on. Reach out to your mentor to ask for prayer and support.

MANAGING SELF

UNDER NEW MANAGEMENT

MARK 7:24-37

[24] Jesus left that place and went to the vicinity of Tyre. He entered a house and did not want anyone to know it; yet he could not keep his presence secret. [25] In fact, as soon as she heard about him, a woman whose little daughter was possessed by an impure spirit came and fell at his feet. [26] The woman was a Greek, born in Syrian Phoenicia.

She begged Jesus to drive the demon out of her daughter. [27] "First let the children eat all they want," he told her, "for it is not right to take the children's bread and toss it to the dogs." [28] "Lord," she replied, "even the dogs under the table eat the children's crumbs." [29] Then he told her, "For such a reply, you may go; the demon has left your daughter." ³⁰ She went home and found her child lying on the bed, and the demon gone. ³¹ Then Jesus left the vicinity of Tyre and went through Sidon, down to the Sea of Galilee and into the region of the Decapolis. ³² There some people brought to him a man who was deaf and could hardly talk, and they begged Jesus to place his hand on him. ³³ After he took him aside, away from the crowd, Jesus put his fingers into the man's ears. Then he spit and touched the man's tongue.

³⁴ He looked up to heaven and with a deep sigh said to him, "Ephphatha!" (which means "Be opened!"). ³⁵ At this, the man's ears were opened, his tongue was loosened and he began to speak plainly. ³⁶ Jesus commanded them not to tell anyone. But the more he did so, the more they kept talking about it. ³⁷ People were overwhelmed with amazement. "He has done everything well," they said. "He even makes the deaf hear and the mute speak."

MARK 8 : 1 - 1 3

---

¹ During those days another large crowd gathered. Since they had nothing to eat, Jesus called his disciples to him and said, ² "I have compassion for these people; they have already been with me three days and have nothing to eat. ³ If I send them home hungry, they will collapse on the way, because some of them have come a long distance."

⁴ His disciples answered, "But where in this remote place can anyone get enough bread to feed them?"

⁵ "How many loaves do you have?" Jesus asked. "Seven," they replied.

⁶ He told the crowd to sit down on the ground. When he had taken the seven loaves and given thanks, he broke them and gave them to his disciples to distribute to the people, and they did so.

⁷ They had a few small fish as well; he gave thanks for them also and told the disciples to distribute them. ⁸ The people ate and were satisfied. Afterward the disciples picked up seven basketfuls of broken pieces that were left over. ⁹ About four thousand were present. After he had sent them away, ¹⁰ he got into the boat with his disciples and went to the region of Dalmanutha. ¹¹ The Pharisees came and began to question Jesus. To test him, they asked him for a sign from heaven. ¹² He sighed deeply and said, "Why does this generation ask for a sign? Truly I tell you, no sign will be given to it." ¹³ Then he left them, got back into the boat and crossed to the other side.

SESSION QUESTIONS

—

WEEK FOUR

DAY 01   Read through the passage for this week from chapters 7 & 8 of the Gospel of Mark. Notice the three miracles performed by Jesus. Is there a common theme or lesson? What can you learn about His power, ability and methods from what you read?

DAY 02   Jump ahead and read Peter's confession of Christ in Mark 8:27-30. Then compare it to the story of the woman from Tyre in 7:24-30. Do her actions and attitudes indicate an understanding of Jesus' identity like Peter did? Do the actions and attitudes you have when you face a concerning situation reveal your belief in Jesus? If so, how? If not, how could they?

DAY 03   Chapter 8:2 says that Jesus had "compassion" on the people. Look for this emotion as you read the rest of chapter 8. Look up the following verses: Isaiah 49:8-13; Psalm 103: 8-13; 116:1-7; 119:73-77. Considering what the Scripture says about God's attitude toward you when you have a great need/desire, how can you turn to and rest in His promises?

DAY 04   When you hurt, what's the one thing you want? For it to stop, right? Nothing unusual about that! While it's natural to focus on what you want when you feel pain, the New Testament offers us a different perspective. Find 2 Cor. 1:3-7 to get a better understanding of how God intends to leverage your difficulty in the lives of others. With this in mind, go to Him in prayer and offer your pain to the Lord for Him to use as He wishes.

DAY 05   Go carefully through Mark 8:31-38. What does Jesus say is in the way of fully following Him? (vs34) For you personally, what does "denying yourself" involve? How can you "take up your cross," (that is, maintain the mindset and mission of Jesus) as you go about your daily routine?

UNDER NEW MANAGEMENT

MANAGING YOUR INFLUENCE

MARK 9:14-50

[14] When they came to the other disciples, they saw a large crowd around them and the teachers of the law arguing with them. [15] As soon as all the people saw Jesus, they were overwhelmed with wonder and ran to greet him.

[16] "What are you arguing with them about?" he asked. [17] A man in the crowd answered, "Teacher, I brought you my son, who is possessed by a spirit that has robbed him of speech. [18] Whenever it seizes him, it throws him to the ground. He foams at the mouth, gnashes his teeth and becomes rigid. I asked your disciples to drive out the spirit, but they could not." [19] "You unbelieving generation," Jesus replied, "how long shall I stay with you? How long shall I put up with you? Bring the boy to me." [20] So they brought him. When the spirit saw Jesus, it immediately threw the boy into a convulsion. He fell to the ground and rolled around, foaming at the mouth. [21] Jesus asked the boy's father,

"How long has he been like this?" "From childhood," he answered. [22] "It has often thrown him into fire or water to kill him. But if you can do anything, take pity on us and help us." [23] "'If you can'?" said Jesus. "Everything is possible for one who believes." [24] Immediately the boy's father exclaimed, "I do believe; help me overcome my unbelief!"

[25] When Jesus saw that a crowd was running to the scene, he rebuked the impure spirit. "You deaf and mute spirit," he said, "I command you, come out of him and never enter him again."

[26] The spirit shrieked, convulsed him violently and came out. The boy looked so much like a corpse that many said, "He's dead." [27] But Jesus took him by the hand and lifted him to his feet, and he stood up. [28] After Jesus had gone indoors, his disciples asked him privately, "Why couldn't we drive it out?"

[29] He replied, "This kind can come out only by prayer." [33] They came to Capernaum. When he was in the house, he asked them, "What were you arguing about on the road?"

[34] But they kept quiet because on the way they had argued about who was the greatest. [35] Sitting down, Jesus called the Twelve and said, "Anyone who wants to be first must be the very last, and the servant of all." [36] He took a little child whom he placed among them. Taking the child in his arms, he said to them, [37] "Whoever welcomes one of these little children in my name

welcomes me; and whoever welcomes me does not welcome me but the one who sent me." [38] "Teacher," said John, "we saw someone driving out demons in your name and we told him to stop, because he was not one of us."

[39] "Do not stop him," Jesus said. "For no one who does a miracle in my name can in the next moment say anything bad about me, [40] for whoever is not against us is for us. [41] Truly I tell you, anyone who gives you a cup of water in my name because you belong to the Messiah will certainly not lose their reward. [42] "If anyone causes one of these little ones—those who believe in me—to stumble, it would be better for them if a large millstone were hung around their neck and they were thrown into the sea. [43] If your hand causes you to stumble, cut it off. It is better for you to enter life maimed than with two hands to go into hell, where the fire never goes out. [45] And if your foot causes you to stumble, cut it off. It is better for you to enter life crippled than to have two feet and be thrown into hell. [47] And if your eye causes you to stumble, pluck it out. It is better for you to enter the kingdom of God with one eye than to have two eyes and be thrown into hell, [48] where "'the worms that eat them do not die, and the fire is not quenched.' [49] Everyone will be salted with fire.

[50] "Salt is good, but if it loses its saltiness, how can you make it salty again? Have salt among yourselves, and be at peace with each other."

SESSION QUESTIONS

—

WEEK FIVE

DAY 01 Read the section from Mark 9 for this week. Summarize the problem that sur-rounded the father of the boy who was demon possessed and what happened to resolve it. Consider what impact this incident likely had on the people watching. Relate this to situations that require you to act in faith when you are in the pres-ence of others.

DAY 02 According to verses 33-34, the disciples were concerned about how they stacked up against each other. Read the response of Jesus here and in Mark 10:35-45 when the issue comes up again. Can you apply what He said to the attitude to "get ahead" and "look out for yourself" that exists in the culture and working world today?

DAY 03 Beginning in verse 38, read the rest of Mark 9. Sometimes we allow (or invite) things into our lives (relationships, material possessions, coping mechanisms) that seem as critically important to us as a hand or foot, but in reality they are contrary to a life of faith. Obviously, Jesus isn't speaking about literal amputation here, but considering the powerful influence our lives can have on others, He is saying that we should be radical in dealing with personal sin. Spend some time thinking and praying over this passage, yielding yourself to the guidance of the Holy Spirit.

DAY 04 Move on to Mark 10. In verses 13-15, Jesus rebukes the disciples for literally blocking the children from coming to Him. Thinking about this story in a more metaphorical sense, how might Christians "hinder" others from coming to Jesus? (read Phil 2:14-16 and James 1:19-2:13) How can you use your influence to draw others to Christ's embrace?

DAY 05 Wrap up this week by reading the story of the Rich Young Ruler in Mark 10:17-31. Resist pushing the story of this man aside supposing it's only about greed and wealth. Look a little more closely to see what Jesus says to you about anything that may be in the way of a deeper relationship with Him. Compare verse 21 to what you read in Matt 4:19-20; 9:9; John 1:43-51. What made the difference in how each of these people responded? Considering what Jesus did in and through his disciples, think of some things that the young ruler may have given up to hold on to his wealth. How can this story challenge you to loosen your grip on possessions, habits, relationships that stand in the way of wholeheartedly following Jesus and impacting the world for Him?

Read the rest of Mark 10 & 11 this weekend.

MANAGING YOUR MONEY

MARK 12:1-44

[1] Jesus then began to speak to them in parables: "A man planted a vineyard. He put a wall around it, dug a pit for the winepress and built a watchtower. Then he rented the vineyard to some farmers and moved to another place. [2] At harvest time he sent a servant to the tenants to collect from them some of the fruit of the vineyard. [3] But they seized him, beat him and sent him away empty-handed. [4] Then he sent another servant to them; they struck this man on the head and treated him shamefully. [5] He sent still another, and that one they killed. He sent many others; some of them they beat, others they killed. [6] "He had one left to send, a son, whom he loved. He sent him last of all, saying, 'They will respect my son.' [7] "But the tenants said to one another, 'This is the heir. Come, let's kill him, and the inheritance will be ours.' [8] So they took him and killed him, and threw him out of the vineyard. [9] "What then will the owner of the vineyard do? He will come and kill those tenants and give the vineyard to others. [10] Haven't you read this passage of Scripture: "'The stone the builders rejected has become the cornerstone; [11] the Lord has done this, and it is marvelous in our eyes'?" [12] Then the chief priests, the teachers of the law and the elders looked for a way to arrest him because they knew he had spoken the

parable against them. But they were afraid of the crowd; so they left him and went away. [13] Later they sent some of the Pharisees and Herodians to Jesus to catch him in his words. [14] They came to him and said, "Teacher, we know that you are a man of integrity. You aren't swayed by others, because you pay no attention to who they are; but you teach the way of God in accordance with the truth. Is it right to pay the imperial tax to Caesar or not? [15] Should we pay or shouldn't we?" But Jesus knew their hypocrisy. "Why are you trying to trap me?" he asked. "Bring me a denarius and let me look at it." [16] They brought the coin, and he asked them, "Whose image is this? And whose inscription?" "Caesar's," they replied. [17] Then Jesus said to them, "Give back to Caesar what is Caesar's and to God what is God's." And they were amazed at him. [18] Then the Sadducees, who say there is no resurrection, came to him with a question. [19] "Teacher," they said, "Moses wrote for us that if a man's brother dies and leaves a wife but no children, the man must marry the widow and raise up offspring for his brother. [20] Now there were seven brothers. The first one married and died without leaving any children. [21] The second one married the widow, but he also died, leaving no child. It was the same with the third. [22] In fact, none of the seven left any children. Last of all, the woman died too. [23] At the resurrection whose wife will she be, since the seven were married to her?" [24] Jesus replied, "Are you not in error because you do not know the Scriptures or the power of God? [25] When the dead rise, they will neither marry nor be given in marriage; they will be like the angels in heaven. [26] Now about the dead rising—have you not read in the Book of Moses, in the account of the burning bush, how God said to him, 'I am the God of Abraham, the God of Isaac, and the God of Jacob'? [27] He is not the God of the dead, but of the living. You are badly mistaken!"

[28] One of the teachers of the law came and heard them debating. Noticing that Jesus had given them a good answer, he asked him, "Of all the commandments, which is the most important?" [29] "The most important one," answered Jesus, "is this: 'Hear, O Israel: The Lord our God, the Lord is one. [30] Love the Lord your God with all your heart and with all your soul and with all your mind and with all your strength.' [31] The second is this: 'Love your neighbor as yourself.' There is no commandment greater than these." [32] "Well said, teacher," the man replied. "You are right in saying that God is one and there is no other but him. [33] To love him with all your heart, with all your understanding and with all your strength, and to love your neighbor as yourself is more important than all burnt offerings and sacrifices." [34] When Jesus saw that he had answered wisely, he said to him, "You are not far from the kingdom of God." And from then on no one dared ask him any more questions.

[35] While Jesus was teaching in the temple courts, he asked, "Why do the teachers of the law say that the Messiah is the son of David? [36] David himself, speaking by the Holy Spirit, declared:"'The Lord said to my Lord: "Sit at my right hand until I put your enemies under your feet."' [37] David himself calls him 'Lord.' How then can he be his son?" The large crowd listened to him with delight. [38] As he taught, Jesus said, "Watch out for the teachers of the law. They like to walk around in flowing robes and be greeted with respect in the marketplaces, [39] and have the most important seats in the synagogues and the places of honor at banquets. [40] They devour widows' houses and for a show make lengthy prayers. These men will be punished most severely." [41] Jesus sat down opposite the place where the offerings were put and watched the crowd putting their money into the temple treasury. Many rich people threw in large amounts. [42] But a poor widow came and put in two very small copper coins, worth only a few cents. [43] Calling his disciples to him, Jesus said, "Truly I tell you, this poor widow has put more into the treasury than all the others. [44] They all gave out of their wealth; but she, out of her poverty, put in everything—all she had to live on."

SESSION QUESTIONS

WEEK SIX

01 So, how are your finances? Do you have enough in retirement? Are you investing in God's kingdom with the resources you have? Have you developed a good balance between spending, saving and giving? If you stiffen a little bit as you read those questions, you're not alone. The topic of money is probably the least favorite topic for Christians, but God's Word is actually full of instruction on the wise use of the resources that God has given us. Read Mark 12, noting anything that it says that can be related to your finances.

02 Focus on what Jesus said about paying taxes to Caesar in verses 13-17. Look up Gen. 1:26-27; 5:1-2; Ps. 139:13-14; Eph. 4:22-24; Col. 3:10. Considering what you read, whose image is imprinted on you? Journal the application of Mark 12:17.

03 Turn to Matthew 25:14-30. The parable Jesus told in this passage addresses all kinds of gifts and talents that are given to us by God, but it definitely speaks directly to our financial resources as well. Read through it carefully and write in your journal what you believe God would have you do to be a good manager and better investor of what He's entrusted to your care. (Think beyond typical investment strategies or retirement plans to include use of your resources to invest in people and kingdom activities.)

04 Look up Romans 13:1-10. What does Paul say about how your relationship to Jesus should play out related to the government, authority figures, taxes and debt owed to others? How does following these verses honor God? Look up some basic information on Emperor Nero to get a better understanding of the kind of authority that was in power in Rome at the time Paul wrote these instructions.

05 Conclude by reading Mark 12:28-34. Relate what Jesus said in verse 30-31 to the topic of your finances and material resources. In a very practical way, how can you more faithfully love God and others with what He has entrusted to you?

MANAGING YOUR PERSPECTIVE

UNDER NEW MANAGEMENT

MARK 13:26-31

²⁶ "At that time people will see the Son of Man coming in clouds with great power and glory. ²⁷ And he will send his angels and gather his elect from the four winds, from the ends of the earth to the ends of the heavens. ²⁸ "Now learn this lesson from the fig tree: As soon as its twigs get tender and its leaves come out, you know that summer is near. ²⁹ Even so, when you see these things happening, you know that it is near, right at the door. ³⁰ Truly I tell you, this generation will certainly not pass away until all these things have happened. ³¹ Heaven and earth will pass away, but my words will never pass away.

SESSION QUESTIONS

———

WEEK SEVEN

DAY 01 What would you do if you knew the future? How would that knowledge change the way you lived right now? Would it impact your priorities and relationships? How about the way you spent your time, money or leisure pursuits? While we can't really know the specifics of every event that lies ahead, Jesus did tell us a little about what to expect in the days to come. Read through Mark 13. Journal your initial thoughts about the warnings outlined here.

DAY 02 The words of Jesus paint a rather bleak picture of the events that will lead up to His return, but His intent wasn't to cause apprehension. Read back through this chapter and underline the messages of hope and encouragement that are sprinkled throughout the chapter. How can what He says make a difference when you encounter opposition to faith in God on your job, and among your family and friends?

DAY 03 The source material for Mark's Gospel most likely came from Peter, Jesus' boldest disciple. (Reread the introduction to the Book of Mark at the beginning of this session for a refresher.) Peter also wrote about the coming "Day of the Lord" in his own letter to the early Christians. Compare what you read in Mark 13 with what you read in 2 Peter 3. What new insights, challenges and/or assurances does Peter add?

DAY 04 Read back through 2 Peter 3, focusing your attention on verses 11-14. How would you answer his question in verse 11? What needs to change for your life to reflect the answer Peter gives to that question? Be specific. (See also, Eph. 5:8-20; 2 Tim. 2:20-26)

DAY 05 Mark 13, 2 Peter 3 and all the other passages in scripture that deal with Christ's return have sparked a lot of debate over the centuries, but instead of worrying about how or when these things might happen, respond to these topics with a more basic question... "So how does this affect me?" Go back to your journal entry from day 1 and add some concrete action points around the certainty of Jesus' return and how these truths can impact your perspective about life right here and right now.

MANAGING YOUR TIME

MARK 14:1-41

UNDER NEW MANAGEMENT

[1] Now the Passover and the Festival of Unleavened Bread were only two days away, and the chief priests and the teachers of the law were scheming to arrest Jesus secretly and kill him. [2] "But not during the festival," they said, "or the people may riot." [3] While he was in Bethany, reclining at the table in the home of Simon the Leper, a woman came with an alabaster jar of very expensive perfume, made of pure nard. She broke the jar and poured the perfume on his head. [4] Some of those present were saying indignantly to one another, "Why this waste of perfume? [5] It could have been sold for more than a year's wages and the money given to the poor." And they rebuked her harshly. [6] "Leave her alone," said Jesus. "Why are you bothering her? She has done a beautiful thing to me. [7] The poor you will always have with you, and you can help them any time you want. But you will not always have me. [8] She did what she could. She poured perfume on my body beforehand to prepare for my burial. [9] Truly I tell you, wherever the gospel is preached throughout the world, what she has done will also be told, in memory of her." [10] Then Judas Iscariot,

one of the Twelve, went to the chief priests to betray Jesus to them. [11] They were delighted to hear this and promised to give him money. So he watched for an opportunity to hand him over. [12] On the first day of the Festival of Unleavened Bread, when it was customary to sacrifice the Passover lamb, Jesus' disciples asked him, "Where do you want us to go and make preparations for you to eat the Passover?" [13] So he sent two of his disciples, telling them, "Go into the city, and a man carrying a jar of water will meet you. Follow him. [14] Say to the owner of the house he enters, 'The Teacher asks: Where is my guest room, where I may eat the Passover with my disciples?' [15] He will show you a large room upstairs, furnished and ready. Make preparations for us there." [16] The disciples left, went into the city and found things just as Jesus had told them. So they prepared the Passover. [17] When evening came, Jesus arrived with the Twelve. [18] While they were reclining at the table eating, he said, "Truly I tell you, one of you will betray me—one who is eating with me."

[19] They were saddened, and one by one they said to him, "Surely you don't mean me?" [20] "It is one of the Twelve," he replied, "one who dips bread into the bowl with me. [21] The Son of Man will go just as it is written about him. But woe to that man who betrays the Son of Man! It would be better for him if he had not been born." [22] While they were eating, Jesus took bread, and when he had given thanks, he broke it and gave it to his disciples, saying, "Take it; this is my body." [23] Then he took a cup, and when he had given thanks, he gave it to them, and they all drank from it. [24] "This is my blood of the covenant, which is poured out for many," he said to them. [25] "Truly I tell you, I will not drink again from the fruit of the vine until that day when I drink it new in the kingdom of God." [26] When they had sung a hymn, they went out to the Mount of Olives. [27] "You will all fall away,"

Jesus told them, "for it is written: "'I will strike the shepherd, and the sheep will be scattered.' [28] But after I have risen, I will go ahead of you into Galilee."

[29] Peter declared, "Even if all fall away, I will not." [30] "Truly I tell you," Jesus answered, "today—yes, tonight—before the rooster crows twice you yourself will disown me three times." [31] But Peter insisted emphatically, "Even if I have to die with you, I will never disown you." And all the others said the same.

[32] They went to a place called Gethsemane, and Jesus said to his disciples, "Sit here while I pray." [33] He took Peter, James and John along with him, and he began to be deeply distressed and troubled. [34] "My soul is overwhelmed with sorrow to the point of death," he said to them. "Stay here and keep watch."

[35] Going a little farther, he fell to the ground and prayed that if possible the hour might pass from him. [36] "Abba, Father," he said, "everything is possible for you. Take this cup from me. Yet not what I will, but what you will." [37] Then he returned to his disciples and found them sleeping. "Simon," he said to Peter, "are you asleep? Couldn't you keep watch for one hour? [38] Watch and pray so that you will not fall into temptation. The spirit is willing, but the flesh is weak." [39] Once more he went away and prayed the same thing. [40] When he came back, he again found them sleeping, because their eyes were heavy. They did not know what to say to him. [41] Returning the third time, he said to them, "Are you still sleeping and resting? Enough! The hour has come. Look, the Son of Man is delivered into the hands of sinners."

SESSION QUESTIONS

———

DAY 01 The significance of time spent on a day's tasks is often evaluated by the visible outcome, but that's rarely a good indicator of actual worth. Mark 14 describes the events of perhaps the most important week in all eternity. While we can see the weight of what Jesus and the disciples were doing, there are other people who contributed as well. Read verses 1-26 and imagine what ordinary things had to happen to prepare for these extraordinary moments. [For example, someone baked the bread, served the meal, greeted the guests, even raised the sheep or made the serving dishes for the party at Simon's house (vs 3) and for Passover (vs 12).] Write down your thoughts as to how you can begin to do the ordinary things in your day for an extraordinary purpose. Read Col. 3:17 out loud. Memorize it this week if you didn't do that in Session 1.

DAY 02 Read verses 27-42. In the Garden of Gethsemane, the disciples missed the significance of what was happening with Jesus even though He came to them for prayer and support three separate times. Often we miss spiritually relevant opportunities because things that are of interest aren't always that important and things that are important aren't always that interesting. Think about that a little. Then, consider what has your attention and is taking up your time that's also getting in the way of the call of Jesus. In prayer, ask Him to show you what needs to be changed.

DAY 03 In his book, 7 Principles of Highly Effective People, Steven Covey writes time management is really a misnomer – the challenge is not to manage time, but to manage ourselves." Journal your response to this statement. Include how this concept is even more important to embrace for believers in Christ. (2 Tim. 1:7 NIV) What self-management strategies can you implement that can assist you in the better use your time? Begin to practice one of them this week.

DAY 04 The world is full of busyness and activity to the point where we feel guilty if we aren't doing something all the time. Look up Mark 6:30-31. Who's suggestion was it to rest? What does that tell you about its value and importance? Take some time to ponder what "rest" really is. Is it different from sleep? From watching Netflix? From planned leisure activities? Make it a point to schedule rest time in your upcoming week and honor its importance by not filling that space with more "pressing" activities.

DAY 05 Find Eph. 5:15-16 in the King James' Version. What's the difference between managing time and redeeming it? How can you make this transition in the way you think about the time you have and what you do with it?

Read the rest of Mark 14 this weekend.

TRUSTING GOD WITH THE OUTCOME

MARK 15:33-47 – 16:1-7

³³At noon, darkness came over the whole land until three in the afternoon. ³⁴ And at three in the afternoon Jesus cried out in a loud voice, "Eloi, Eloi, lema sabachthani?" (which means "My God, my God, why have you forsaken me?") ³⁵ When some of those standing near heard this, they said, "Listen, he's calling Elijah." ³⁶ Someone ran, filled a sponge with wine vinegar, put it on a staff, and offered it to Jesus to drink. "Now leave him alone. Let's see if Elijah comes to take him down," he said. ³⁷ With a loud cry, Jesus breathed his last. ³⁸ The curtain of the temple was torn in two from top to bottom. ³⁹ And when the centurion, who stood there in front of Jesus, saw how he died he said, "Surely this man was the Son of God!" ⁴⁰ Some women were watching from a distance. Among them were Mary Magdalene, Mary the mother of James the younger and of Joseph, and Salome. ⁴¹ In Galilee these women had followed him and cared for his needs. Many other women who had come up with him to Jerusalem were

UNDER NEW MANAGEMENT

also there. [42] It was Preparation Day (that is, the day before the Sabbath). So as evening approached, [43] Joseph of Arimathea, a prominent member of the Council, who was himself waiting for the kingdom of God, went boldly to Pilate and asked for Jesus' body. [44] Pilate was surprised to hear that he was already dead. Summoning the centurion, he asked him if Jesus had already died. [45] When he learned from the centurion that it was so, he gave the body to Joseph. [46] So Joseph bought some linen cloth, took down the body, wrapped it in the linen, and placed it in a tomb cut out of rock. Then he rolled a stone against the entrance of the tomb. [47] Mary Magdalene and Mary the mother of Joseph saw where he was laid.

MARK 16: 1-7

[1] When the Sabbath was over, Mary Magdalene, Mary the mother of James, and Salome bought spices so that they might go to anoint Jesus' body. [2] Very early on the first day of the week, just after sunrise, they were on their way to the tomb [3] and they asked each other, "Who will roll the stone away from the entrance of the tomb?" [4] But when they looked up, they saw that the stone, which was very large, had been rolled away. [5] As they entered the tomb, they saw a young man dressed in a white robe sitting on the right side, and they were alarmed. [6] "Don't be alarmed," he said. "You are looking for Jesus the Nazarene, who was crucified. He has risen! He is not here. See the place where they laid him. [7] But go, tell his disciples and Peter, 'He is going ahead of you into Galilee. There you will see him, just as he told you.'"

SESSION QUESTIONS

—

WEEK NINE

01 Open up this week's session by reading all of Mark 15 & 16. Sit with the story for a moment. Breathe in the enormity of what Jesus voluntarily endured so that your sin might be forgiven. Journal your thoughts.

02 Think about how wrong the events of the crucifixion must have felt to the disciples and the objections they undoubtedly voiced as they unfolded. Compare what you read yesterday to what you find in Psalm 22. What comfort, encouragement or reassurance can you draw from knowing that the crucifixion and resurrection were so precisely planned by God so long before it actually happened? Can you apply this to the confusing and bewildering things that happen in your world? How?

03 Mary Magdalene is mentioned in Mark 15:40, 47 & in 16:1-10. Scripture says Jesus appeared to her first after His resurrection. Imagine what Mary's life was like before and after meeting Jesus based on what you read in Mark 16:9 and Luke 8:1-3. Considering the depth of despair and darkness of her life before meeting Jesus and how her life changed, why do you think she was the perfect choice for Jesus to reveal Himself to first? Write down a little of your conversion story and how it can be an encouragement to trust God even when your world seems dark and full of despair.

04 Since the section at the end of Mark (16:9-20) doesn't appear in the oldest known manuscripts and has some differences in writing style, some scholars believe this section was added to conclude the account in a manner consistent with the other Gospel writers. Other experts disagree with the objections and hold to the authenticity of the entire passage. Read this section and compare it to what you find in Matthew 28. What challenge for living today do you take away from both accounts?

05 Go back to the beginning of this session and reread the introduction. Skim through your notes and revisit anything that was particularly impacting from this study. Especially consider what you discovered about the power, authority and mission of Jesus in these eight weeks. What changes have you made (or do you need to make) now that you realize that your life is "under new management?"

BEAUTY FROM ASHES

BEAUTY FROM ASHES

Matthew 11 contains one of the most difficult stories in the whole New Testament. The events that unfold in these verses cause us to wrestle and ask some hard questions. John the Baptizer or Baptist, as most of us know him, is on the scene. He shows up early in the Gospels preaching an uncompromising message of repentance that caught the attention of the masses and stirred the ire of the religious leaders of the day (Matt. 3:1-12; Luke 3:1-18). However, his public clash with Herod over his adulterous and wicked lifestyle landed John in a Roman jail for nearly two years (Lk 3: 19-20; Matt 11:2). As the months of imprisonment wore on, John sent his followers to ask Jesus a pointed and puzzling question. "Are you the one who is to come, or should we expect someone else?" (Matt 11:3) Huh? Isn't this the guy who was God's chosen prophet to prepare the way for Jesus? Isn't he the one who clearly identified Jesus as "Lamb of God, who takes away the sin of the world?" (John 1:29) That's the Gospel message in one statement. If anyone knew that Jesus was "the One," it was John, right? And yet here in these verses John is wrestling with some questions. Now, go three more chapters into Matthew, and the situation gets worse when John is brutally killed and mocked (Matt 14:1-12). There is part of all of us when we read this story, we just don't think it seems to end right. It's difficult not to wonder where the "save the day" moment for John was. Wasn't Jesus paying attention to what was happening to him? Just one word from Jesus and the plot could have changed.

Perhaps you know exactly what that feels like. You're following Jesus and expected life to turn out one way, and it just hasn't ended up "right." Sickness stole something from you. Sin broke something. Selfishness of others took something away that can never be returned. Dreams failed. As you try to make sense of your story, have you found yourself silently wondering something very close to what John asked? Is Jesus "the One" or should you expect someone else? There are certainly no simple answers to eliminate all the desperate questions that surface after tragedy and heartache shatter long-held dreams, but as we wrestle with Matthew 11 and look carefully at Jesus's answer to John, it may help us hold on to faith when we feel ourselves sink into a prison of despair. "Go

back and report to John what you hear and see: The blind receive sight, the lame walk, those who have leprosy are cleansed, the deaf hear, the dead are raised, and the good news is proclaimed to the poor." (Matt. 11:4-5)In this one sentence, Jesus paraphrased the prophecy from Isaiah 61 and through it reminded John, and us, to widen our vision. Jesus affirmed John's faith by telling him to look at the evidence and to trust what he knew to be true. That is, the prophecy of God was being fulfilled just as it was written. This truth challenges us to examine the basis of our belief as well. Are we followers of Christ because of what He does for us? Or are we followers because we know who He is and what he has already DONE for us?

Some will suffer great trials and disappointment and be eventually exalted like Joseph (Gen. 41). Others, like John, will suffer disappointment and the earthly happy ending won't come (Matt 14:1-12). BUT, the truth of the Gospel is that no matter what we face, God will not, can not, does not, leave us here to endure alone. Our perfect, loving Savior is greater than any of the unexplained circumstances that come our way. As His children, we can trust that no matter how disappointing or confusing our situation, He always births beauty from the ashes of calamity (Rom. 8:28). Yes, it may take a while for us to see it, and we may never see it this side of heaven, but even still we can anchor our lives in the assurances of Scripture and know that Jesus is - and forever will be - worthy of our hope, praise, and life. Even in the darkest days.

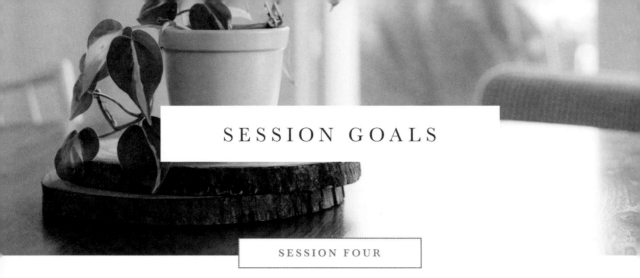

SESSION GOALS

BEAUTY FROM ASHES

GOALS

- To help us see our disappointments and lost dreams in context of the sovereignty of God and as of use to Him for divine purposes.

- To affirm our conviction to do the right and godly thing even when it may cost us something.

- To guide us to embrace our opportunities and see ourselves as positioned in our current situation "for such a time as this." (Esther 4:14)

- To help us develop the skill of waiting on the Lord for His timing.

QUESTIONS

- God doesn't always reveal Himself in obvious ways. How have you seen Him move in the background of your life?

- What beautiful things in your life have grown out of the ashes of disappointment or heartache?

- What have you learned that can help you face future disappointments with confidence in God?

- Sometimes we play the role of Esther. Sometimes we are called to be like Mordecai. To whom can you be an encourager?

- How can you be the voice of faith in even impossible situations?

INTRO TO ESTHER

What if there was a moment in your life that could change your future forever? One that would solidify your purpose and give your existence spiritual meaning and impact that would reverberate through many lives? Would you take it? Most of us would say "yes" without hesitation. But what if taking that opportunity also meant giving up a deeply held dream, or enduring heartache and pain or giving up something precious in the process? Would you still say "yes" so quickly?

This session we'll look at the book of Esther as an example of a woman whose life took a different turn than she expected. Her dedication to God and willingness to risk everything in a crucial time in the life of Israel stands as a constant reminder to us to be faithful to Jesus and give ourselves fully to His purposes regardless our circumstances.

As we jump into this ancient story to look for modern impact, let's set the scene. Long before Esther appeared in Susa (present day Iran, Esther 1:2), Jerusalem was overrun and the city burned by the Babylonians under the rule of Nebuchadnezzar (Jer. 52:12-13). The Jews who survived the assault were hauled away from their homeland, taken into captivity [as prophesied by the prophet Jeremiah (Jer. 23:11)] and held as slaves in this foreign land. Decades later, Cyrus the Great led the Persians to conquer the Babylonian Empire (just as it was foretold in Is. 45). In the first year of his reign, the new ruler issued a decree to rebuild Jerusalem and, in somewhat of a unique declaration, abolished slavery in all forms in his kingdom. Thank you, Cyrus! Among other things, these edicts allowed exiled Jews to return to their homeland. (The books of Nehemiah and Ezra tell the story of the restoration of the city wall and construction of a new temple.)

However, despite their newfound freedom, only about 50,000 Jews chose to return to their former land, while the majority stayed put. Fast forward 50 more years and we land on the grandson of Cyrus, King Xerxes I,

(known to the Jews as Ahasuerus). He was a powerful ruler with a kingdom spreading from India to modern day Ethiopia (Esther 1:1). Unsatisfied with his empire as it was and determined to complete the failed objective of his father, he became solely focused on conquering the Greeks. In his third year as sovereign, he invited his personal officials, as well as military leaders, princes and nobles from across his realm to a huge gathering with the probable intention of enticing them to join his military campaign (1:3-4).

But instead of being a massive party given only for the purpose of indulgence, this assembly was likely comprised of a lengthy and grand display of Persian might and included strategic planning sessions mapping out the invasion of Greece. The extravagant festival ultimately resulted in the banishment of Xerxes wife, Queen Vashti (1:19).

Enter: Esther. Hers is a story that rivals the best Hollywood has to offer. Political scheming. Desperate beauty. Power and betrayal. Courage in the face of death. All set against the backdrop of grandeur of one of the most impressive kingdoms of all time.

For the next 8 weeks, we will soak in the story of an unlikely hero who risked it all to save her people. In the process, we are invited to learn from the example of this brave woman and yield our own desperation to Jesus. Esther's faithful devotion to God and courage in the face of extreme trial exemplifies the character and strength it takes to posture ourselves in the position of surrender and say to God, "Here I am. Send me." (Is. 6:8)

DECISIONS, DECISIONS

—

ESTHER 1

BEAUTY FROM ASHES

[1] This is what happened during the time of Xerxes, the Xerxes who ruled over 127 provinces stretching from India to Cush: [2] At that time King Xerxes reigned from his royal throne in the citadel of Susa, [3] and in the third year of his reign he gave a banquet for all his nobles and officials. The military leaders of Persia and Media, the princes, and the nobles of the provinces were present. [4] For a full 180 days he displayed the vast wealth of his kingdom and the splendor and glory of his majesty. [5] When these days were over, the king gave a banquet, lasting seven days, in the enclosed garden of the king's palace, for all the people from the least to the greatest who were in the citadel of Susa. [6] The garden had hangings of white and blue linen, fastened with cords of white linen and purple material to silver rings on marble pillars. There were couches of gold and silver on a mosaic pavement of porphyry, marble, mother-of-pearl and other costly stones. [7] Wine was served in goblets of gold, each one different from the other, and the royal wine was abundant, in keeping with the king's liberality. [8] By the king's command each guest was allowed to drink with no restrictions, for the king instructed all the wine stewards to serve each man what he wished. [9] Queen Vashti also gave a banquet for the women in the royal palace of King Xerxes. [10] On the seventh day,

when King Xerxes was in high spirits from wine, he commanded the seven eunuchs who served him—Mehuman, Biztha, Harbona, Bigtha, Abagtha, Zethar and Karkas— [11] to bring before him Queen Vashti, wearing her royal crown, in order to display her beauty to the people and nobles, for she was lovely to look at. [12] But when the attendants delivered the king's command, Queen Vashti refused to come. Then the king became furious and burned with anger. [13] Since it was customary for the king to consult experts in matters of law and justice, he spoke with the wise men who understood the times [14] and were closest to the king—Karshena, Shethar, Admatha, Tarshish, Meres, Marsena and Memukan, the seven nobles of Persia and Media who had special access to the king and were highest in the kingdom. [15] "According to law, what must be done to Queen Vashti?" he asked. "She has not obeyed the command of King Xerxes that the eunuchs have taken to her."[16] Then Memukan replied in the presence of the king and the nobles, "Queen Vashti has done wrong, not only against the king but also against all the nobles and the peoples of all the provinces of King Xerxes.[17] For the queen's conduct will become known to all the women, and so they will despise their husbands and say, 'King Xerxes commanded Queen Vashti to be brought before him, but she would not come.' [18] This very day the Persian and Median women of the nobility who have heard about the queen's conduct will respond to all the king's nobles in the same way. There will be no end of disrespect and discord. [19] "Therefore, if it pleases the king, let him issue a royal decree and let it be written in the laws of Persia and Media, which cannot be repealed, that Vashti is never again to enter the presence of King Xerxes. Also let the king give her royal position to someone else who is better than she. [20] Then when the king's edict is proclaimed throughout all his vast realm, all the women will respect their husbands, from the least to the greatest." [21] The king and his nobles were pleased with this advice, so the king did as Memukan proposed. [22] He sent dispatches to all parts of the kingdom, to each province in its own script and to each people in their own language, proclaiming that every man should be ruler over his own household, using his native tongue.

SESSION QUESTIONS

—

WEEK ONE

DAY 01 Read the story of King Xerxes and Vashti in Esther 1. The Queen faced an impossible choice. She could submit and be paraded through a party of drunken foreigners. Or she could refuse and risk execution. While most of us will never face such a dire situation, we do have to make decisions that can have long term effects and far reaching impact on ourselves and others. Spend a few minutes honestly considering your answers to some basic questions about decision making:

Do I tend to act impulsively or routinely consider the long term consequences?
How much do feelings matter in what I decide?
How impacting are my past experiences on my present decision making process?
Do I seek godly counsel regularly?
Am I most interested in eternal impact or what seems best right now?

DAY 02 Wise decisions begin with…well, wisdom! Compare the two metaphorical women introduced in Proverbs 9. How are they alike? Different? How can you tell the two apart when you're in a situation where you have to make an immediate decision?

DAY 03 Vashti was certainly not a believer in the one true God, and we don't know all the details surrounding her decision and ultimate banishment, but sometimes even good and godly people suffer as a result of the decisions of others. Turn to Genesis 37 to be reminded of one such person.

DAY 04 Continue reading the story of Joseph in Genesis 39. What advantages could he have afforded himself if he'd have said "yes" to the offer? Theorize how he might have rationalized this decision (ex. No one will know, God doesn't care about me, etc). How do you counter the temptation to rationalize clearly wrong decisions? What does his perspective (vs 9) teach you about doing the right thing even when you might have to risk something?

DAY 05 Starting in chapter 37, skim through the rest of Genesis, making a quick list of the injustices and hardships that Joseph endured at the hands of others (Brothers, jailer, Potiphar's wife etc). Read Genesis 50:15-21. Thinking back through all that's happened to you as a result of the decisions of others, how does it change your perception if you, by faith, pronounce verse 20 over them?

CHANGE OF PLANS

—

ESTHER 2

The tendency is to read Esther 2 as a direct chronological continuation of chapter 1 and assume that the fury of King Xerses was as a result of the actions of Queen Vashti, but if you look a little closer and mix in a little bit of history, a different picture comes into focus. A careful reading of the text reveals that about three years elapsed between chapter 1 & 2 (Esther 1:3 & 2:16). During that span, the Persian Empire invaded Greece (reread: Intro to Esther) and after a ground war that lasted a year's time, both sides had suffered significant losses. If we bypass all the places, names and dates that mean little to most people and jump to the end, records tell us that the tide of the conflict ultimately turned in favor of the outnumbered Greeks during the naval Battle of Salamis. Unable to move efficiently in the narrowed waters between the mainland and the island, the Persian fleet suffered a huge defeat at the hands of the smaller, and more mobile Greek ships. Xerxes helplessly watched the destruction from the shore, then retreated in disgust at his military's failure, leaving only a small force behind in Greece. They, too, were eventually defeated a short time later bringing the final end to the Second Persian War.

¹ Later when King Xerxes' fury had subsided, he remembered Vashti and what she had done and what he had decreed about her. ² Then the king's personal attendants proposed, "Let a search be made for beautiful young virgins for the king. ³ Let the king appoint commissioners in every province of his realm to bring all these beautiful young women into the harem at the citadel of Susa. Let them be placed under the care of Hegai, the king's eunuch, who is in charge of the women; and let beauty treatments be given to them. ⁴ Then let the young woman who pleases the king be queen instead of Vashti." This advice appealed to the king, and he followed it.⁵ Now there was in the citadel of Susa a Jew of the tribe of Benjamin, named Mordecai son of Jair, the son of Shimei, the son of Kish, ⁶ who had been carried into exile from Jerusalem by Nebuchadnezzar king of Babylon, among those taken captive with Jehoiachin king of Judah. ⁷ Mordecai had a cousin named Hadassah, whom he had brought up because she had neither father nor mother. This young woman, who was also known as Esther, had a lovely figure and was beautiful. Mordecai had taken her as his own daughter when her father and mother died. ⁸ When the king's order and edict had been proclaimed, many young women were brought to the citadel of Susa and put under the care of Hegai. Esther also was taken to the king's palace and entrusted to Hegai, who had charge of the harem. ⁹ She pleased him and won his favor. Immediately he provided her with her beauty treatments and special food. He assigned to her seven female attendants selected from the king's palace and moved her and her attendants into the best place in the harem. ¹⁰ Esther had not revealed her nationality and family background, because Mordecai had forbidden her to do so. ¹¹ Every day he walked back and forth near the courtyard of the harem to find out how Esther was and what was happening to her. ¹² Before a young woman's turn came to go in to King Xerxes, she had to complete twelve months of beauty treatments prescribed for the women, six months with oil of myrrh and six with perfumes and cosmetics.¹³ And this is how she would go to the king: Anything she wanted was given her to take with her from the harem to the king's palace. ¹⁴ In the evening she would go there and in the morning

return to another part of the harem to the care of Shaashgaz, the king's eunuch who was in charge of the concubines. She would not return to the king unless he was pleased with her and summoned her by name. [15] When the turn came for Esther (the young woman Mordecai had adopted, the daughter of his uncle Abihail) to go to the king, she asked for nothing other than what Hegai, the king's eunuch who was in charge of the harem, suggested. And Esther won the favor of everyone who saw her. [16] She was taken to King Xerxes in the royal residence in the tenth month, the month of Tebeth, in the seventh year of his reign. [17] Now the king was attracted to Esther more than to any of the other women, and she won his favor and approval more than any of the other virgins. So he set a royal crown on her head and made her queen instead of Vashti. [18] And the king gave a great banquet, Esther's banquet, for all his nobles and officials. He proclaimed a holiday throughout the provinces and distributed gifts with royal liberality. [19] When the virgins were assembled a second time, Mordecai was sitting at the king's gate. [20] But Esther had kept secret her family background

and nationality just as Mordecai had told her to do, for she continued to follow Mordecai's instructions as she had done when he was bringing her up. [21] During the time Mordecai was sitting at the king's gate, Bigthana and Teresh, two of the king's officers who guarded the doorway, became angry and conspired to assassinate King Xerxes. [22] But Mordecai found out about the plot and told Queen Esther, who in turn reported it to the king, giving credit to Mordecai.[23] And when the report was investigated and found to be true, the two officials were impaled on poles. All this was recorded in the book of the annals in the presence of the king.

SESSION QUESTIONS

—

DAY 01　From what you read last week, and what you now see in chapter 2, jot down a few of King Xerxes character traits. Reread vs 8-14 which detail what amounts to an elaborate beauty contest, only in this case, the prize was marriage to a drunken, womanizing pagan king. (The losers were consigned to the king's haram, without the opportunity to ever have husbands or families of their own.) Think about what this meant to Esther's hopes and dreams as a Hebrew girl. However, she willingly submitted. Are there dreams that God may be asking you to surrender to fulfill His calling on your life?

DAY 02　Go carefully through chapter 2 again, looking for anything that shows God's activity behind the scenes as Esther is moved in to position as Queen of Persia. How does this encourage you when you face a perplexing situation?

DAY 03　Look at verses 9-10; 15-16; 20. What do these reveal about Esther's character? Make notes about what 1 Sam. 16:7; 2 Cor. 4:16-17; and 1 Peter 3:3-4 tell you about how to emulate a similar kind of attractiveness.

DAY 04　Thinking about what you know about the story so far, read Psalm 31. Can you see how truths such as these (which she may have been exposed to through Mordecai) could have been what helped Esther thrive in her less than ideal situation? How can they give you encouragement when circumstances send you in a direction that seems to be far from where you had hoped your life would be? Memorize vs. 14-15a.

DAY 05　Read the last section of chapter 2, beginning in verse 19. Notice that God not only positioned Esther in a prominent place, but did the same with Mordecai. Survey your life for a moment. How have you seen God orchestrate people, places, and events in your world to accomplish His plan? [Don't forget to think specifically about how you came to faith in Christ, and all the people (pastors, authors, teachers, friends, family, etc) who were used to bring the Gospel to you.] End this week in thankful prayer and a willing heart to give yourself to His use in the lives of others.

BEAUTY FROM ASHES

A CONFLICT ARISES

—

ESTHER 3

[1] After these events, King Xerxes honored Haman son of Hammedatha, the Agagite, elevating him and giving him a seat of honor higher than that of all the other nobles. [2] All the royal officials at the king's gate knelt down and paid honor to Haman, for the king had commanded this concerning him. But Mordecai would not kneel down or pay him honor.

[3] Then the royal officials at the king's gate asked Mordecai, "Why do you disobey the king's command?" [4] Day after day they spoke to him but he refused to comply. Therefore they told Haman about it to see whether Mordecai's behavior would be tolerated, for he had told them he was a Jew. [5] When Haman saw that Mordecai would not kneel down or pay him honor, he was enraged. [6] Yet having learned who Mordecai's people were, he scorned the idea of killing only Mordecai. Instead Haman looked for a way to destroy all Mordecai's people, the Jews, throughout the whole kingdom of Xerxes. [7] In the twelfth year of King Xerxes, in the first month, the month of Nisan, the pur (that is, the lot) was cast in the presence of Haman to select a day and month. And the lot fell on[a] the twelfth month, the month of Adar.

8 Then Haman said to King Xerxes, "There is a certain people dispersed among the peoples in all the provinces of your kingdom who keep themselves separate. Their customs are different from those of all other people, and they do not obey the king's laws; it is not in the king's best interest to tolerate them. 9 If it pleases the king, let a decree be issued to destroy them, and I will give ten thousand talents[b]of silver to the king's administrators for the royal treasury."10 So the king took his signet ring from his finger and gave it to Haman son of Hammedatha, the Agagite, the enemy of the Jews. 11 "Keep the money," the king said to Haman, "and do with the people as you please."12 Then on the thirteenth day of the first month the royal secretaries were summoned. They wrote out in the script of each province and in the language of each people all Haman's orders to the king's satraps, the governors of the various provinces and the nobles of the various peoples. These were written in the name of King Xerxes himself and sealed with his own ring. 13 Dispatches were sent by couriers to all the king's provinces with the order to destroy, kill and annihilate all the Jews—young and old, women and children—on a single day, the thirteenth day of the twelfth month, the month of Adar, and to plunder their goods. 14 A copy of the text of the edict was to be issued as law in every province and made known to the people of every nationality so they would be ready for that day. 15 The couriers went out, spurred on by the king's command, and the edict was issued in the citadel of Susa. The king and Haman sat down to drink, but the city of Susa was bewildered.

By the time we come to this chapter, Esther is well established in her new role and has served as queen for around four years. Little is known about her first experiences, but we can be sure that they were radically different from anything she'd known before her elevation to this public role. Amid the elegance and ceremony that swirled around her royal position, there was one thing that did remain from her former life. Her relationship with Mordecai. Though her station in life was far above his, she maintained her connection and relied on his advice. In this section of scripture, we'll see a tense relationship between Mordecai and the king's honored official, Haman develop in to an explosive confrontation.

SESSION QUESTIONS

—

WEEK THREE

DAY 01 Sometimes the past can be important for understanding relationships in the present. That dynamic is relevant in this chapter of Esther's story. After reading through the entire section, go back to verse 1-2 to notice the ancestry of Haman. As an 'Agagite', he was directly related to King Agag. Read 1 Samuel 15 to find out more about Haman's predecessor.

DAY 02 Go back to Esther 2:5 to learn a little about Mordecai's heritage. Look up 1 Samuel 9:1-2 to find a common name in both passages. Knowing Mordecai's family relationship and based on what you read yesterday, read Esther 3:1-6 again. What insight does that background give to the conflict that existed generally between Amalekites and Jews and specifically between Haman and Mordecai? Consider any deeply rooted family issues that continue to impact your relationships today. How and why do they remain relevant?
(For more background on the animosity between the Jews and Amalekites see: Gen 36:12, 16; Ex 17:8-15; Deut. 25:17-19; Num. 14:36-45; Jud. 6:1-5)

DAY 03 Mordecai was pressured to bow to Haman, but he refused compromise. Have you ever felt compelled to 'bow' to the opinions or actions of others? Make notes on what you find in 1 Peter 3:10-17 that will help you stand strong when you feel coerced to compromise.

DAY 04 Go through Esther 3:7-15. At this point in the story, the situation for Mordecai and the rest of the Jews seemed dire. Jesus warned that days like these would come again. (Matt 24 & 25) Read Luke 12:4-11 to find encouragement to remain faithful. Write down the promises that are most reassuring to you.

DAY 05 Commitment to Jesus sometimes causes irreconcilable conflict with people around us. Matthew 19: 27-30 reminds us that our sacrifices for Him are never overlooked or in vain. End this week with prayer, asking God to give you the strength to stand firm in your devotion to Him.

FOR SUCH A TIME AS THIS

—

ESTHER 4

BEAUTY FROM ASHES

[1] When Mordecai learned of all that had been done, he tore his clothes, put on sackcloth and ashes, and went out into the city, wailing loudly and bitterly. [2] But he went only as far as the king's gate, because no one clothed in sackcloth was allowed to enter it. [3] In every province to which the edict and order of the king came, there was great mourning among the Jews, with fasting, weeping and wailing. Many lay in sackcloth and ashes. [4] When Esther's eunuchs and female attendants came and told her about Mordecai, she was in great distress. She sent clothes for him to put on instead of his sackcloth, but he would not accept them. [5] Then Esther summoned Hathak, one of the king's eunuchs assigned to attend her, and ordered him to find out what was troubling Mordecai and why. [6] So Hathak went out to Mordecai in the open square of the city in front

of the king's gate. [7] Mordecai told him everything that had happened to him, including the exact amount of money Haman had promised to pay into the royal treasury for the destruction of the Jews. [8] He also gave him a copy of the text of the edict for their annihilation, which had been published in Susa, to show to Esther and explain it to her, and he told him to instruct her to go into the king's presence to beg for mercy and plead with him for her people.[9] Hathak went back and reported to Esther what Mordecai had said. [10] Then she instructed him to say to Mordecai, [11] "All the king's officials and the people of the royal provinces know that for any man or woman who approaches the king in the inner court without being summoned the king has but one law: that they be put to death unless the king extends the gold scepter to them and spares their lives. But thirty days have passed since I was called to go to the king." [12] When Esther's words were reported to Mordecai, [13] he sent back this answer: "Do not think that because you are in the king's house you alone of all the Jews will escape. [14] For if you remain silent at this time, relief and deliverance for the Jews will arise from another place, but you and your father's family will perish. And who knows but that you have come to your royal position for such a time as this?" [15] Then Esther sent this reply to Mordecai: [16] "Go, gather together all the Jews who are in Susa, and fast for me. Do not eat or drink for three days, night or day. I and my attendants will fast as you do. When this is done, I will go to the king, even though it is against the law. And if I perish, I perish." [17] So Mordecai went away and carried out all of Esther's instructions.

SESSION QUESTIONS

———

WEEK FOUR

DAY 01 If cell phones had existed in the days of this story, the bulk of chapter 4 would basically be a text exchange between Esther and Mordecai concerning Haman's plot to destroy the Jews. Notice the variety of responses to the edict in issued at the end of chapter 3. (3:15; 4:1-3) How have you seen widely differing attitudes occur to the same situation?

DAY 02 Go back through chapter 4:9-13. Look at Esther's initial response to Mordecai's instructions. What was the basis for her reluctance? As a believer in Christ, you don't have to fear the wrath of an unpredictable king. Look up John 3:36; Rom. 3:22-24, 5:9; 1 Thess. 5:8-11. Note what they say about God's attitude toward those who know Jesus. Memorize Heb. 4:15-16 and keep it as a reminder of your "all access" pass into the presence of the King of kings!

DAY 03 Flip over to Daniel 3:1-30 to read about three other people who were in an impossible situation somewhat similar to Esther's. Notice the phrase "even if he does not" in verse 18. Their expectation was that a stand for God was about to turn out very badly for them too. If you are facing a situation with an uncertain outcome, get a clean note card and write out a commitment of faithfulness to God regardless of how it turns out. Put a date by it and tuck it in your Bible as a reminder of your devotion to Jesus.

DAY 04 Chapter 4:14 is the turning point of Esther's life. Until this moment she seemed to be just the unlikely trophy wife of a pagan king. But God had her positioned perfectly for "such a time as this." Where have you been positioned to make a big impact in someone's life? Work? Home? School? Consider how you might be used by God in unlikely places too, like in a cancer treatment center, at the unemployment office, or in a lawyer's office. Spend some time in prayer asking for Jesus to give you the courage to make the most of your opportunities. Read Isaiah 43:1-3, 10-13.

"I can't do it because _____." Esther could have filled in the blank with a lot of realistic reasons for inaction, but in faith, she turned her concern away from herself, toward her people, and ultimately, trusted God with the results. Make a list of what you might be tempted to put in that blank (ex. I can't because of my background, because I have young children, because I don't have the right education, etc). Tear your list up and in prayer, symbolically lay it before God. Set aside your reasons for hesitation and offer yourself fully to God for His use.

BEAUTY FROM ASHES

TIMING IS EVERYTHING

—

ESTHER 5

[1] On the third day Esther put on her royal robes and stood in the inner court of the palace, in front of the king's hall. The king was sitting on his royal throne in the hall, facing the entrance. [2] When he saw Queen Esther standing in the court, he was pleased with her and held out to her the gold scepter that was in his hand. So Esther approached and touched the tip of the scepter. [3] Then the king asked, "What is it, Queen Esther? What is your request? Even up to half the kingdom, it will be given you."

[4] "If it pleases the king," replied Esther, "let the king, together with Haman, come today to a banquet I have prepared for him." [5] "Bring Haman at once," the king said, "so that we may do what Esther asks." So the king and Haman went to the banquet Esther had prepared. [6] As they were drinking wine, the king again asked Esther, "Now what is your petition? It will be given you. And what is your request? Even up to half the kingdom, it will be granted." [7] Esther replied, "My petition and my request is this: [8] If the king regards me with favor and if it pleases the king to grant my petition and fulfill my request, let the king and Haman come tomorrow to the banquet I will prepare for them. Then I will answer the king's question." [9] Haman went out that day happy and in high spirits. But when he saw Mordecai at the king's gate and observed that he neither rose nor showed fear in his presence, he was filled with rage against Mordecai. [10] Nevertheless, Haman restrained himself and went home.

Calling together his friends and Zeresh, his wife, [11] Haman boasted to them about his vast wealth, his many sons, and all the ways the king had honored him and how he had elevated him above the other nobles and officials. [12] "And that's not all," Haman added. "I'm the only person Queen Esther invited to accompany the king to the banquet she gave. And she has invited me along with the king tomorrow. [13] But all this gives me no satisfaction as long as I see that Jew Mordecai sitting at the king's gate." [14] His wife Zeresh and all his friends said to him, "Have a pole set up, reaching to a height of fifty cubits, and ask the king in the morning to have Mordecai impaled on it. Then go with the king to the banquet and enjoy yourself." This suggestion delighted Haman, and he had the pole set up.

SESSION QUESTIONS

—

WEEK FIVE

DAY 01

Are you facing a difficult situation that seems to have no good solution? Before you take someone's advice or decided what to do on your own, go back to Esther 4:15-17. Notice what she did before chapter 5 begins. Whether you choose to fast or not, remember the importance of seeking God before you make decisions and surrendering the results to Him. (Review Week 7, day 4 from last session). Read Isaiah 26:3-8, then spend some focused time in prayer, asking for God's guidance and peace.

DAY 02

Read through chapter 5, taking note of Esther's attitude toward the king. She exemplifies how we should show respect and honor to those placed in authority over us (even when they aren't Christ followers). Make notes about what you find in 1 Peter 2:13-23.

DAY 03

The threat against the Jews was very real. The king's mood could have changed at any moment. It was a desperate situation, but in chapter 5, Esther seemed to take the long way around to get to what she wanted. However, as you look further in the story, you can see that God had a strategy which He was unfolding behind the scenes. Turn over to Psalm 37:1-9 and look for encouragement to be patient and stick with God's plan even when difficult situations seem to push you to move quickly.

DAY 04

Waiting on God's timing is essential to walking in His will – even when it may seem like time is running out. Look up 1 Samuel 13:5-14. Notice the words "I saw" "I thought" & "I felt" in Saul's justification for his actions (vs 11-12, NIV). Instead of acting on external appearances or internal emotions, what should be your criteria for making decisions? (Jos. 1:7-9; Prov. 3:5-6; John 8:32, 14:23-24; Rom. 12:2; Phil. 4:6-7; 2 Tim 3:16-17)

DAY 05

Go back to read Esther 5:9-14, then turn over to Titus 3:3 to see how believers once were capable of character very much like Haman. (Look up a definition of malice if you need it.) Keep reading through verse 7 to see what changed. End this week with grateful prayer.

BEAUTY FROM ASHES

SLEEPLESS IN SUSA

ESTHER 6

[1] That night the king could not sleep; so he ordered the book of the chronicles, the record of his reign, to be brought in and read to him. [2] It was found recorded there that Mordecai had exposed Bigthana and Teresh, two of the king's officers who guarded the doorway, who had conspired to assassinate King Xerxes. [3] "What honor and recognition has Mordecai received for this?" the king asked. "Nothing has been done for him," his attendants answered. [4] The king said, "Who is in the court?" Now Haman had just entered the outer court of the palace to speak to the king about impaling Mordecai on the pole he had set up for him. [5] His attendants answered, "Haman is standing in the court." "Bring him in," the king ordered. [6] When Haman entered, the king asked him, "What should be done for the man the king delights to honor?" Now Haman thought to himself, "Who is there that the king would rather honor than me?" [7] So he answered the king,

"For the man the king delights to honor, [8] have them bring a royal robe the king has worn and a horse the king has ridden, one with a royal crest placed on its head. [9] Then let the robe and horse be entrusted to one of the king's most noble princes. Let them robe the man the king delights to honor, and lead him on the horse through the city streets, proclaiming before him, 'This is what is done for the man the king delights to honor!'" [10] "Go at once," the king commanded Haman. "Get the robe and the horse and do just as you have suggested for Mordecai the Jew, who sits at the king's gate. Do not neglect anything you have recommended." [11] So Haman got the robe and the horse. He robed Mordecai, and led him on horseback through the city streets, proclaiming before him, "This is what is done for the man the king delights to honor!" [12] Afterward Mordecai returned to the king's gate. But Haman rushed home, with his head covered in grief, [13] and told Zeresh his wife and all his friends everything that had happened to him. His advisers and his wife Zeresh said to him, "Since Mordecai, before whom your downfall has started, is of Jewish origin, you cannot stand against him—you will surely come to ruin!" [14] While they were still talking with him, the king's eunuchs arrived and hurried Haman away to the banquet Esther had prepared.

SESSION QUESTIONS

———

WEEK SIX

_{DAY} 01   Read Psalm 73:12-13. When have you felt like this? What encouragement concerning the justice of God can you draw from the events of Esther 6? End your time by reading Psalm 73:27-28.

_{DAY} 02   Flip back to Esther 2:21-23 to remind yourself of what Mordecai did on behalf of Xerxes. Several years has elapsed by the time we get to chapter 6. Can you see the reason for the delayed recognition? Write down any take-away that you can hold on to when there appears to be delays in God's plan.

_{DAY} 03   God progressed His plan through a bout of insomnia (Esther 6:1). Consider how the restlessness that you sometimes feel could actually be the whisper God uses to move you forward into His will for your life. Journal your response to Psalm 119:148.

_{DAY} 04   How are the events concerning Mordecai and Haman from this chapter predicted in Psalm 101? Spend some time thinking about any upcoming decisions you have to make. Ask God to help you realize any underlying motivations you may not be aware of.

_{DAY} 05   Answer the question from yesterday after reading Psalm 125. Even if you haven't seen the deliverance of God in your situation yet, consciously look for the ways "the Lord surrounds" you to remind you that He hasn't forgotten you.

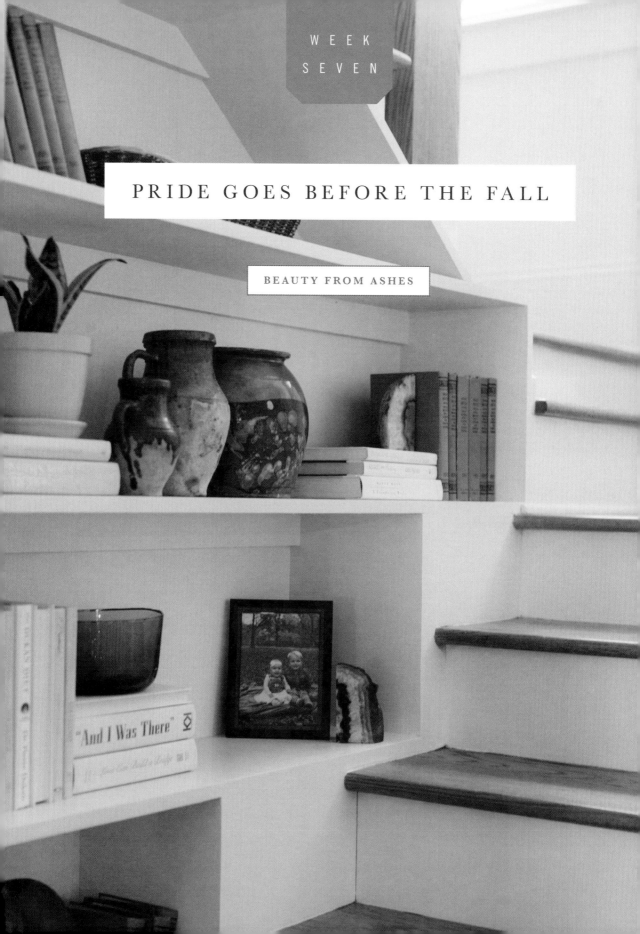

PRIDE GOES BEFORE THE FALL

BEAUTY FROM ASHES

¹ So the king and Haman went to Queen Esther's banquet, ² and as they were drinking wine on the second day, the king again asked, "Queen Esther, what is your petition? It will be given you. What is your request? Even up to half the kingdom, it will be granted." ³ Then Queen Esther answered, "If I have found favor with you, Your Majesty, and if it pleases you, grant me my life— this is my petition. And spare my people— this is my request. ⁴ For I and my people have been sold to be destroyed, killed and annihilated. If we had merely been sold as male and female slaves, I would have kept quiet, because no such distress would justify disturbing the king." ⁵ King Xerxes asked Queen Esther, "Who is he? Where is he— the man who has dared to do such a thing?" ⁶ Esther said, "An adversary and enemy! This vile Haman!" Then Haman was terrified before the king and queen. ⁷ The king got up in a rage, left his wine and went out into the palace garden. But Haman, realizing that the king had already decided his fate, stayed behind to beg Queen Esther for his life. ⁸ Just as the king returned from the palace garden to the banquet hall, Haman was falling on the couch where Esther was reclining. The king exclaimed, "Will he even molest the queen while she is with me in the house?" As soon as the word left the king's mouth, they covered Haman's face. ⁹ Then Harbona, one of the eunuchs attending the king, said, "A pole reaching to a height of fifty cubits stands by Haman's house. He had it set up for Mordecai, who spoke up to help the king." The king said, "Impale him on it!" ¹⁰ So they impaled Haman on the pole he had set up for Mordecai. Then the king's fury subsided.

SESSION QUESTIONS

—

WEEK SEVEN

DAY 01 Can you see the incredible irony in the events of Esther 6 & 7 and how Haman's own self-importance led to his destruction? Read Isaiah 2:11-22, noting what God says about pride. Remember to include the tendency to trust in yourself in the caution found in vs 22.

DAY 02 Turn to Daniel 4 to read the story of Nebuchadnezzar's pride. How did God warn him? What happened as a result of his unwillingness to listen? How is this like the story of Haman? How is it different?

DAY 03 Let's make Esther 7 personal. If you consider Haman to be symbolic of the part of each of us that seeks to exalt itself, what does Romans 6:5-14 say our response to it should be? (vs 11-14)

DAY 04 How do the things listed in 1 John 2:15-16 work together to lead believers away from God? Think about how things that you crave, lust after, or boast in have affected your heart for Jesus.

DAY 05 It's easy to see an unjust situation and try to manipulate the circumstances to make it work out the way we want it too. What do you learn from Esther and Haman in this chapter that will help you trust the Lord and wait for His plan to unfold? See Ecc. 12:13-14; Gal. 6:7-9.

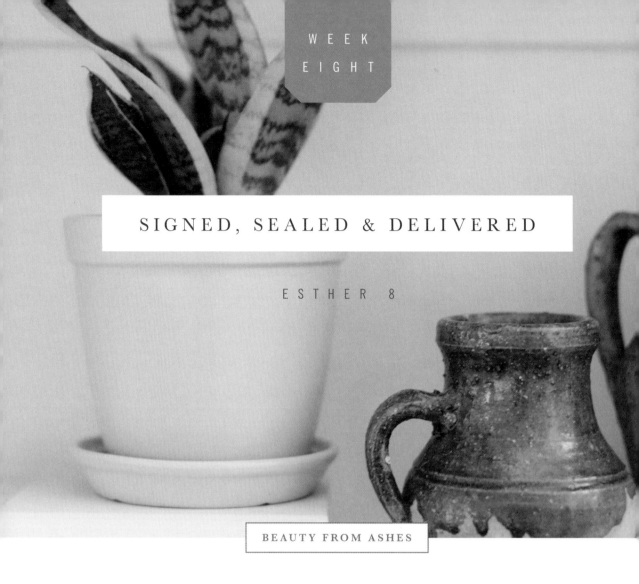

SIGNED, SEALED & DELIVERED

ESTHER 8

BEAUTY FROM ASHES

[1] That same day King Xerxes gave Queen Esther the estate of Haman, the enemy of the Jews. And Mordecai came into the presence of the king, for Esther had told how he was related to her. [2] The king took off his signet ring, which he had reclaimed from Haman, and presented it to Mordecai. And Esther appointed him over Haman's estate. [3] Esther again pleaded with the king, falling at his feet and weeping. She begged him to put an end to the evil plan of Haman the Agagite, which he had devised against the Jews. [4] Then the king extended the gold scepter to Esther and she arose and stood before him.

[5] "If it pleases the king," she said, "and if he regards me with favor and thinks it the right thing to do, and if he is pleased with me, let an order be written overruling the dispatches that Haman son of Hammedatha, the Agagite, devised and wrote to destroy the Jews in all the king's prov-

inces. [6] For how can I bear to see disaster fall on my people? How can I bear to see the destruction of my family?" [7] King Xerxes replied to Queen Esther and to Mordecai the Jew, "Because Haman attacked the Jews, I have given his estate to Esther, and they have impaled him on the pole he set up. [8] Now write another decree in the king's name in behalf of the Jews as seems best to you, and seal it with the king's signet ring—for no document written in the king's name and sealed with his ring can be revoked." [9] At once the royal secretaries were summoned—on the twenty-third day of the third month, the month of Sivan. They wrote out all Mordecai's orders to the Jews, and to the satraps, governors and nobles of the 127 provinces stretching from India to Cush. These orders were written in the script of each province and the language of each people and also to the Jews in their own script and language. [10] Mordecai wrote in the name of King Xerxes, sealed the dispatches with the king's signet ring, and sent them by mounted couriers, who rode fast horses especially bred for the king. [11] The king's edict granted the Jews in every city the right to assemble and protect themselves; to destroy, kill and annihilate the armed men of any nationality or province who might attack them and their women and children, and to plunder the property of their enemies. [12] The day appointed for the Jews to do this in all the provinces of King Xerxes was the thirteenth day of the twelfth month, the month of Adar. [13] A copy of the text of the edict was to be issued as law in every province and made known to the people of every nationality so that the Jews would be ready on that day to avenge themselves on their enemies. [14] The couriers, riding the royal horses, went out, spurred on by the king's command, and the edict was issued in the citadel of Susa. [15] When Mordecai left the king's presence, he was wearing royal garments of blue and white, a large crown of gold and a purple robe of fine linen. And the city of Susa held a joyous celebration. [16] For the Jews it was a time of happiness and joy, gladness and honor. [17] In every province and in every city to which the edict of the king came, there was joy and gladness among the Jews, with feasting and celebrating. And many people of other nationalities became Jews because fear of the Jews had seized them.

SESSION QUESTIONS

—

WEEK EIGHT

DAY 01   Esther had been through a lot of stress, turmoil and change by the time we reach chapter 8. How is she different now than she was at the beginning of the story? Think about the biggest crisis of your life. How has it changed you? Write down your thoughts and include how you think God has (or can) use it for His glory.

DAY 02   In verse 3-6, Esther pleads for the lives of her people before the king. Is there anyone you are deeply concerned about? Go to your Righteous King and continue in prayer for that person(s), trusting that He will respond in love. (Ps. 4:1; Rom. 12:12; Jas. 5:16)

DAY 03   Esther 1:19 & 8:8 refer to the laws that once signed by the king couldn't be revoked. Read Romans 5:12, Eph. 2:1-3 to see the irrevocable law of God concerning sin. Then look up Rom. 6:23, 8:1, Eph. 2:4-9 to see God's glorious answer to this 'dilemma.' End your time with thanksgiving for what is yours in Christ!

DAY 04   Read Esther 8:17 to see how the joy of God's deliverance affected the people who lived around the Jews. Look up Romans 15:13 to see what should overflow out of our lives as believers. Prayerfully consider if the hope and joy of Christ is evident to others in your home and workplace.

DAY 05   Even when things aren't going as we'd hoped, Jesus-followers still have many reasons to rejoice. Psalm 136 is a song and a reminder of what God did on behalf of Israel. After reading what the psalmist wrote, copy the first 4 verses in your journal and continue this pattern with at least 4 more personal entries to compose your own choral praise. Make it personal to include the unmistakable things God has done in your life. (Be sure to include New Testament truths that are yours as a believer!) Continue adding to your personal psalm as praises come to your mind.

[17] This happened on the thirteenth day of the month of Adar, and on the fourteenth they rested and made it a day of feasting and joy. [18] The Jews in Susa, however, had assembled on the thirteenth and fourteenth, and then on the fifteenth they rested and made it a day of feasting and joy. [19] That is why rural Jews—those living in villages—observe the fourteenth of the month of Adar as a day of joy and feasting, a day for giving presents to each other. [20] Mordecai recorded these events, and he sent letters to all the Jews throughout the provinces of King Xerxes, near and far, [21] to have them celebrate annually the fourteenth and fifteenth days of the month of Adar [22] as the time when the Jews got relief from their enemies, and as the month when their sorrow was turned into joy and their mourning into a day of celebration. He wrote them to observe the days as days of feasting and joy and giving presents of food to one another and gifts to the poor. [23] So the Jews agreed to continue the celebration they had begun, doing what Mordecai had written to them. [24] For Haman son of Hammedatha, the Agagite, the enemy of all the Jews, had plotted against the Jews to destroy them and had cast the pur (that is, the lot) for their ruin and destruction. [25] But when the plot came to the king's attention, he issued written orders that the evil scheme Haman had devised against the Jews should come back onto his own head, and that he and his sons should be impaled on poles. [26] (Therefore these days were called Purim, from the word pur.) Because of everything written in this letter and because of what they had seen and what had happened to them, [27] the Jews took it on themselves to establish the custom that they and their descendants and all who join them should without fail observe these two days every year, in the way prescribed and at the time appointed. [28] These days should be remembered and observed in every generation by every family, and in every province and in every city. And these days of Purim should never fail to be celebrated by the Jews—nor should the memory of these days die out among their descendants. [29] So Queen Esther, daughter of Abihail, along with Mordecai the Jew, wrote with full authority to confirm this second letter concerning Purim. [30] And Mordecai sent letters to all the Jews in the 127 provinces of Xerxes' kingdom—words of goodwill and assurance— [31] to establish these days of Purim at their designated times, as Mordecai the Jew and Queen Esther had decreed for them, and as they had established for themselves and their descendants in regard to their times of fasting and lamentation. [32] Esther's decree confirmed these regulations about Purim, and it was written down in the records.

ESTHER 10:1-3

[1] King Xerxes imposed tribute throughout the empire, to its distant shores. [2] And all his acts of power and might, together with a full account of the greatness of Mordecai, whom the king had promoted, are they not written in the book of the annals of the kings of Media and Persia? [3] Mordecai the Jew was second in rank to King Xerxes, preeminent among the Jews, and held in high esteem by his many fellow Jews, because he worked for the good of his people and spoke up for the welfare of all the Jews.

SESSION QUESTIONS

—

WEEK NINE

DAY 01   Read through the last chapters of the book of Esther. What happened here? What is Purim and why is it still celebrated today? (vs 20-23)

DAY 02   In the Old Testament, God instituted many weekly, monthly and yearly celebrations and festivals designed to remind followers of His faithfulness and provision. While New Testament believers aren't required to keep those traditions today, we can -and should- make a practice of celebrating how the Lord cares and provides for us. Make a list of at least 5 specific things that Jesus has specifically done for you. How can you celebrate these marvelous works?

DAY 03   Look up Hebrews 13:15 to see one way you can celebrate God's goodness. Notice the word "continually". Think about how you can move your praise for Jesus out of a "Sunday only" activity and into your everyday routine. Continue reading through vs. 18 to see at least 5 other ways you can honor the work of Christ in your life.

DAY 04   Now that we have finished the story of Esther, read John 5:39-40. How does this book "testify" about Jesus?

DAY 05   Many scholars from history questioned whether Esther should have been included in the Bible because it doesn't mention God's name directly. Summarize how you saw God's hand moving in the background throughout the entire story. Write down what you learn from this that will help you in times when Jesus doesn't seem to be on the "front page" of your life.

BE WELCOMED IN THIS PLACE

SESSION FIVE

Have you ever been to a dinner party where everything from the food to the decor looks like it came right off the front page of Pinterest? The table is punctuated with hand-designed floral decorations grown in the host's own garden Immaculately and precisely ornamented furnishings (right down to the cute little bow that adorns the roll of toilet paper in the bathroom) are painstakingly attended to while tempting aromas entice your palate for the feast. Suddenly, the bag of corn chips, jarred salsa and store brand soda you brought seem inadequate and out of place when compared to the exquisitely presented array of food that borders on being a work of art.

Keep that picture in mind and realize that all of us have been sent an invitation to attend God's "party," written in the blood of Jesus Christ and delivered personally by the Holy Spirit. But instead of simply accepting the invitation and entering into the hall to enjoy the lavish generosity of our grand Host, we feel the obligation to add something to the occasion, as if our inadequate contribution will in some way validate our presence there. However, Scripture reminds us that when it comes to being in the presence of our Holy Creator, we can bring nothing to the gathering that will enhance our righteousness (Is. 64:4; Eph. 2:1-5), nor can we in any way enrich what God has so freely offered (Eph. 2:8-9).

Yet, though empty-handed, still we are welcomed.

Instead of allowing feelings of inadequacy to shame you, realize that once you've accepted the invitation from God, you are no longer merely an invited guest, but rather through Christ, have become a valued and loved member of His family. That elevated position insures that you will never hold a second rate status, and that you're not required to pave the way to access into God's presence on your own. Rest in the words of Romans chapter 5: "since we have been justified through faith, we have peace with God through our Lord Jesus Christ, through whom we have gained access by faith into this grace in which we now stand." (vs 1-2)

Christ's sacrifice has granted you entry and this new standing with God imparts a permanent place in the Father's house and access to Him at any time, and for any reason. (Heb. 4:16)

So instead of looking for something good enough to bring to gain the favor of the Lord, it's time to change roles and from your position as a child of God, begin to emulate the great kindness, love, and open heart of Jesus.

It seems unlikely that a man who walked the earth 2000 years ago and lived a meager lifestyle without a permanent home or any significant material possessions could teach us anything about hospitality in the 21st century, but maybe that in itself shows us much about how convoluted our perception of hospitality really is. Could we have inverted the true meaning for so long that we honestly believe what we have is more important than who we are? This session we will sit at the feet of Jesus and learn what it means to truly welcome others into our homes... and into our lives... with the same grace, mercy, and peace that we have first received from the greatest Host of all.

SESSION GOALS

SESSION FIVE

BE WELCOMED IN THIS PLACE

GOALS

- To help us recognize hospitality as a character trait of God.

- To guide us in seeing that true hospitality grows out of a relationship with Jesus.

- To widen the understanding of hospitality, taking it beyond the modern view of simply 'entertaining.'

- To lead us in developing a heart of hospitality that reaches beyond our family and friends.

- To remove common obstacles to opening our lives to others, and to encourage us to offer generosity to others right now.

QUESTIONS

- Often we want to welcome only friends and family. How do you see a different pattern emerging in God's actions toward you?

- What holds you back from or motivates you toward being hospitable and gracious toward others?

- How can you realign your thinking to extend hospitality to others but maintaining an attitude of service and worship of God?

- How can you practically 'love' those who you disagree with or who are difficult to be around?

SESSION FIVE / WEEK ONE

BE WELCOMED IN THIS PLACE

GRACIOUS HOSPITALITY

—

EXODUS 6:1-8

[1] Then the LORD said to Moses, "Now you will see what I will do to Pharaoh. Because of my mighty hand he will let them go; because of my mighty hand he will drive them out of his country." [2] God also said to Moses, "I am the LORD. [3] I appeared to Abraham, to Isaac and to Jacob as God Almighty, but by my name the LORD I did not make myself fully known to them. [4] I also established my covenant with them to give them the land of Canaan, where they resided as foreigners. [5] Moreover, I have heard the groaning of the Israelites, whom the Egyptians are enslaving, and I have remembered my covenant. [6] "Therefore, say to the Israelites: 'I am the LORD, and I will bring you out from under the yoke of the Egyptians. I will free you from being slaves to them, and I will redeem you with an outstretched arm and with mighty acts of judgment. [7] I will take you as my own people, and I will be your God. Then you will know that I am the LORD your God, who brought you out from under the yoke of the Egyptians. [8] And I will bring you to the land I swore with uplifted hand to give to Abraham, to Isaac and to Jacob. I will give it to you as a possession. I am the LORD.'"

"Grace is the hospitality of God to welcome sinners not because of their goodness but because of his glory. If God chose not to magnify the glory of his own self-sufficiency, and instead to enrich himself by looking for talented and virtuous housemates, there would be no grace in the world, and no hospitality, and no salvation. We owe our eternal life to grace, and grace is God's disposition to glorify his freedom and power and wealth by showing hospitality to sinners."

- John Piper // DesiringGod.org

SESSION QUESTIONS

—

WEEK ONE

DAY 01 Read Exodus 6:1-8. Underline every time the name of the Lord is referenced. From this exercise, what can you conclude is the motivation for God's activity on behalf of Israel?

DAY 02 Based on what you read yesterday, what was the status of Israel in the land of Egypt? Read King David's prayer in 2 Samuel 7:22-24, noting the change in designation after they left Egypt.

DAY 03 God made a home for Israel and took them fully into His own family. Look up Psalm 106:1-8 to find the Lord's motivation for freeing Israel from bondage. Why does this matter to us today? (Reread and reflect on the quote from John Piper again)

DAY 04 Move over to Romans 1:1-6. Look for the same phrase you found in Psalm 106:8 yesterday. Use the NIV if your version of the Bible doesn't have a matching phrase. Think about grace and the hospitality of God extended to you as mentioned in verse 5-6. Journal your response.

DAY 05 Hospitality isn't just a girl thing; it's a God thing! Have you ever considered His expression of grace to sinners to be a picture of hospitality before? With this concept in mind, go carefully through Eph. 2:4-22. How does that change your understanding of the importance of this virtue?

SESSION FIVE / WEEK TWO

REJECTED OR WELCOMED

—

ISAIAH 53

[1] Who has believed our message and to whom has the arm of the LORD been revealed? [2] He grew up before him like a tender shoot, and like a root out of dry ground. He had no beauty or majesty to attract us to him, nothing in his appearance that we should desire him. [3] He was despised and rejected by mankind, a man of suffering, and familiar with pain. Like one from whom people hide their faces he was despised, and we held him in low esteem. [4] Surely he took up our pain and bore our suffering, yet we considered him punished by God, stricken by him, and afflicted. [5] But he was pierced for our transgressions, he was crushed for our iniquities; the punishment that brought us peace was on him, and by his wounds we are healed. [6] We all, like sheep, have gone astray, each of us has turned to our own way; and the LORD has laid on him the iniquity of us all. [7] He was oppressed and afflicted, yet he did not open his mouth; he was led like a lamb to the slaughter, and as a sheep before its shearers is silent, so he did not open his mouth. [8] By oppression and judgment he was taken away. Yet who of his generation protested? For he was cut off from the land of the living; for the transgression of my people he was punished. [9] He was assigned a grave with the wicked, and with the rich in his death, though he had done no violence, nor was any deceit in his mouth. [10] Yet it was the LORD's will to crush him and cause him to suffer, and though the LORD makes his life an offering for sin, he will see his offspring and prolong his days, and the will of the LORD will prosper in his hand. [11] After he has suffered, he will see the light of life and be satisfied; by his knowledge my righteous servant will justify many, and he will bear their iniquities. [12] Therefore I will give him a portion among the great, and he will divide the spoils with the strong, because he poured out his life unto death, and was numbered with the transgressors. For he bore the sin of many, and made intercession for the transgressors.

SESSION QUESTIONS

—

WEEK TWO

DAY 01

Jesus is the King of kings and Lord of lords and the Son of God! He created all things and by His power holds all things together (Col 1:16-20). Yet when He came to this earth in human flesh, there was no welcome mat waiting for Him. Read Isaiah 53 to get the prophetic picture of how Jesus was received. Underline any impacting words or phrases.

DAY 02

We looked at Isaiah 55 in session 2. Go back through that chapter again and in light of what you read yesterday, pay attention to the welcoming heart of Jesus and gracious offer made to all people who will come. Add any additional thoughts around the topic of His hospitality in your journal.

DAY 03

From a borrowed womb (Lk. 1:26-38) to a borrowed tomb (Matt. 27:57-61), Jesus was a stranger in the world He created (Matt. 8:20). As you sit in the first 18 verses of John 1, consider the irony of verses 10-11. In spite of the ill treatment given to Christ by those who He created (then and now), see His warm and gracious response in verses 12-13 &16.

DAY 04

Most of us like to think we would pull out the best we have, throw open the door, and spare no expense to greet Jesus. But do we really do that? Look up Matt. 25:31-46 to see what Christ said about attending to Him. How can you graciously welcome Jesus today?

DAY 05

Romans 5:8 reminds us that when we were still sinners (unable to help ourselves in any way), Christ died for us … as a direct and unmistakable demonstration of God's extravagant love. Is there someone that you know who is "unable to help themselves" who needs a tangible expression of God's love? [Since God showed you compassion when you were His enemy, resist the tendency to think only about people who you like and get along with. (Matt. 5:43-48)] Write this person(s) name on a blank card and tape it to your mirror. Every time you see it, ask God to show you how you can express His kind of hospitality to this person. If you can't think of anyone right now, tape a blank card to your mirror and ask God to send someone your way.

BE WELCOMED IN THIS PLACE

CALLED TO LOVE

—

1 JOHN 3 : 11 - 24

[11] For this is the message you heard from the beginning: We should love one another. [12] Do not be like Cain, who belonged to the evil one and murdered his brother. And why did he murder him? Because his own actions were evil and his brother's were righteous. [13] Do not be surprised, my brothers and sisters, if the world hates you. [14] We know that we have passed from death to life, because we love each other. Anyone who does not love remains in death. [15] Anyone who hates a brother or sister is a murderer, and you know that no murderer has eternal life residing in him. [16] This is how we know what love is: Jesus Christ laid down his life for us. And we ought to lay down our lives for our brothers and sisters. [17] If anyone has material possessions and sees a brother or sister in need but has no pity on them, how can the love of God be in that person? [18] Dear children, let us not love with words or speech but with actions and in truth. [19] This is how we know that we belong to the truth and how we set our hearts at rest in his presence: [20] If our hearts condemn us, we know that God is greater than our hearts, and he knows everything. [21] Dear friends, if our hearts do not condemn us, we have confidence before God [22] and receive from him anything we ask, because we keep his commands and do what pleases him. [23] And this is his command: to believe in the name of his Son, Jesus Christ, and to love one another as he commanded us. [24] The one who keeps God's commands lives in him, and he in them. And this is how we know that he lives in us: We know it by the Spirit he gave us.

SESSION QUESTIONS

—

WEEK THREE

DAY 01

A heart of hospitality begins in a relationship with Jesus. By faith, you've been welcomed into His family and adopted as His child (Rom. 8:15)! Gratitude calls us to extend the same kind of love and grace to others. Go through 1 John 3:11-24, underlining anything that stands out about loving those around you.

DAY 02

Sometimes it's easier to show love to acquaintances than it is to the people in our own families. After rereading the passage from yesterday, turn back to Genesis 4:1-16 to refresh yourself on the story of Cain and Abel. Especially take note of Cain's motivation. Is there anger, jealousy or strife that exists between members of your family? Bring these situations to God in prayer. Ask Him to show you how to extend the love of Jesus to these people. (Review 1 Cor. 13) **Bitterness and anger blocks the flow of God's love through us. The beginning point of family restoration may be for you to work through forgiveness in your own heart first (see Matt. 18:21-35; Rom. 12:17-21; Eph. 4:32; Col 3:13). Reach out to your mentor if you have struggles in this area.**

DAY 03

Go back to Genesis 4:6-7. Notice how sin is described. Look up and reread some verses that we looked at in session 2 with regard to spiritual conflict. This time think about these passages in terms of the struggles that occur with those around you… especially in your family. What do 1 Peter 5:8-9; Eph. 6:12-18; 2 Cor. 10:3-6 remind you about where -and with whom- the real fight exists. How can this change the way you perceive and react to discord?

DAY 04

Love is more than warm feelings. Focus on the "new commandment" Jesus gave His followers (you) in John 13:34-35 (repeated in 1 John 3:23). Start a list of some tangible ways Christ has "loved you." How can you extend a similar kind of inviting love to those with whom you interact? Remember that the way we show love to others is the way they know we are related to Jesus.

DAY 05

Look up Romans 1:7 to see how Paul addressed the believers in Rome. Being "loved by God" is a designation, not a feeling. Add "grace" and "peace" to your list from yesterday and include other spiritual treasures that are yours because of Christ's love. Based on His attitude toward you, make some concrete action points about how to open your heart and life to those who are sometimes hard to love.

wonderbread

Eyes opened! Chains broken! Hearts restored! So many death to life stories! It's inspiring to see God explode sweeping world-wide outreaches like our churches and ministries which lift up the name of Jesus and impact the lives of countless people who are in search of the truth all around the globe. Only God can fully know how the prayer, faithfulness and innumerable hours of tireless work continues to show up and show off in thousands of transformed lives every year. While we can (and definitely should) applaud the work of Jesus and highlight the incredible redemptive stories of those that have been touched through this kind of labor, sometimes the large and far reaching impact tends to make those who are behind the scenes and well out of the spotlight feel as though we're perhaps missing something or that maybe our efforts aren't really all that important. Maybe you've often wondered how one weary, worn-out soccer mom… one underpaid and over-worked barista… one highly caffeinated, sleep-deprived college student … could really influence anyone's life, much less make any difference in a world filled with so much want.

But you can! A familiar story in the Gospels gives us this wonderful reminder: Jesus is capable of doing "immeasurably more" with what seems to be very little (Eph 3:20).

"Another of his disciples, Andrew, Simon Peter's brother, spoke up, "Here is a boy with five small barley loaves and two small fish, but how far will they go among so many?" Jesus said, "Have the people sit down." There was plenty of grass in that place, and they sat down (about five thousand men were there). Jesus then took the loaves, gave thanks, and distributed to those who were seated as much as they wanted. He did the same with the fish. - John 6:8-11

Sometimes when we look at the things we have, we're tempted to be a little under-impressed. Our abilities. Our talents. Our stuff. They may not look very substantial, flashy or exciting and in many ways appear more like common fish and bread than anything of great worth. But our assessment of true value is inaccurate, mainly because we make the same mistake that the disciples did when Jesus told them to feed that group of over 5000 people. They assumed because something is small, it is of little or no value for the exceedingly large need. But, they (and we) fail to take into account the transforming power of Christ and His ability to take what we have and do amazing things with it.

What a gift that the little boy who gave his lunch got to see the great miracle that Jesus did on the hillside. Sometimes we get a front row seat to see miracles in our lives, but often we won't get that opportunity. It's in those times that we need to remember that we're called to "live by faith, not by sight" (2 Cor 5:7). We can trust and believe that He will multiply our work, even if we never get to see the mouths that it feeds.

As we continue to move forward in this session and look at ways we can "break bread" with others, keep in mind that no matter how small your "loaf" appears, bring what you have anyway. Your physical wealth, your words or simply your presence, we want to live open-handed with whatever we have. Offer your best to the Lord, and then rest in the confident knowledge that all it takes is the touch of the Master to make a massive impact in the Kingdom of God.

PRACTICE MAKES PERMANENT

—

ROMANS 12:9-21

[9] Love must be sincere. Hate what is evil; cling to what is good. [10] Be devoted to one another in love. Honor one another above yourselves. [11] Never be lacking in zeal, but keep your spiritual fervor, serving the Lord. [12] Be joyful in hope, patient in affliction, faithful in prayer. [13] Share with the Lord's people who are in need. Practice hospitality. [14] Bless those who persecute you; bless and do not curse. [15] Rejoice with those who rejoice; mourn with those who mourn. [16] Live in harmony with one another. Do not be proud, but be willing to associate with people of low position. Do not be conceited.[17] Do not repay anyone evil for evil. Be careful to do what is right in the eyes of everyone. [18] If it is possible, as far as it depends on you, live at peace with everyone. [19] Do not take revenge, my dear friends, but leave room for God's wrath, for it is written: "It is mine to avenge; I will repay," says the Lord. [20] On the contrary: "If your enemy is hungry, feed him; If he is thirsty, give him something to drink. In doing this, you will heap burning coals on his head." [21] Do not be overcome by evil, but overcome evil with good.

SESSION QUESTIONS

—

WEEK FOUR

DAY 01 Read Romans 12:9-21, highlighting verse 13. What comes to mind when you hear the world "hospitality?" How is it different from entertaining? When you notice the smaller word within "hospitality," does it change the images you have? How? The original Greek word is "philoxenia" which means "love to strangers." Does this change your concept even more? Write down your thoughts.

DAY 02 Romans 12 doesn't mention throw pillows, tidy dining spaces, or fancy meals, but it does call us to serve. With your new definition of hospitality in mind from yesterday, reread this passage. Think about how the instructions before and after vs 13 can be incorporated in to a lifestyle of hospitality.

DAY 03 Look up Acts 16:1-15. Lydia is the first recorded convert to Christianity in Europe. What did she do immediately after believing in Jesus? What does your faith compel you to do? What could you do to "persuade" others with your open heart and open doors?

DAY 04 Continuing reading Acts 16 through the end of the chapter. Lydia's house was the likely residence of Paul and his companions for some time (verse 18 says Paul was in Philippi for "many days") and certainly, her home was the gathering place of believers (vs 40). In what ways can you move beyond "entertaining" and "practice hospitality" for the purpose of discipleship, encouragement, and/or worship?

DAY 05 Lydia opened her doors for Paul and his missionary team to teach the Gospel in Philippi. Some Bible experts think her house could have also been the initial meeting place for the fledgling Philippian church, and later Paul's letter to the church may have even been read there. With this back story in mind, read Phil. 4:10-19. How did the early believers continue to express concern for Paul once he left the city? How does that change your understanding of the familiar statement in verse 19? Apply this section of Scripture to the topic of hospitality… especially thinking of how you might continue to be hospitable to people once they leave your home.

BE WELCOMED IN THIS PLACE

ENTERTAINING STRANGERS

—

GENESIS 18:1-14

[1] The Lord appeared to Abraham near the great trees of Mamre while he was sitting at the entrance to his tent in the heat of the day. [2] Abraham looked up and saw three men standing nearby. When he saw them, he hurried from the entrance of his tent to meet them and bowed low to the ground. [3] He said, "If I have found favor in your eyes, my lord,] do not pass your servant by. [4] Let a little water be brought, and then you may all wash your feet and rest under this tree. [5] Let me get you something to eat, so you can be refreshed and then go on your way—now that you have come to your servant." "Very well," they answered, "do as you say." [6] So Abraham hurried into the tent to Sarah. "Quick," he said, "get three seahs] of the finest flour and knead it and bake some bread." [7] Then he ran to the herd and selected a choice, tender calf and gave it to a servant, who hurried to prepare it. [8] He then brought some curds and milk and the calf that had been prepared, and set these before them. While they ate, he stood near them under a tree. [9] "Where is your wife Sarah?" they asked him. "There, in the tent," he said. [10] Then one of them said, "I will surely return to you about this time next year, and Sarah your wife will have a son."

Now Sarah was listening at the entrance to the tent, which was behind him. [11] Abraham and Sarah were already very old, and Sarah was past the age of childbearing. [12] So Sarah laughed to herself as she thought, "After I am worn out and my lord is old, will I now have this pleasure?" [13] Then the Lord said to Abraham, "Why did Sarah laugh and say, 'Will I really have a child, now that I am old?' [14] Is anything too hard for the Lord? I will return to you at the appointed time next year, and Sarah will have a son."

SESSION QUESTIONS

—

DAY 01   The culture and traditions of the Old Testament are very different from the way of life we find ourselves in today. Though a few inns could be found in some cities, there existed nothing like our modern hotels, motels and restaurants. Travelers often had to rely on the hospitality of local residents to find food, shelter and protection. Read through the story of Abraham and the three strangers from Genesis 18. Notice how he treated the visitors. What attitudes motivated his actions?

DAY 02   Read through the passage from Genesis 18 again. Write down the specific things Abraham and Sarah did to make the travelers feel welcome. Beside each, jot down how those things could be translated into a realistic modern equivalent.

DAY 03   Verse 2 says that Abraham "hurried from the entrance of his tent to meet them." Is this your attitude when strangers show up at church, social gatherings or office? Pray for sensitivity and make a point to mimic Abraham's actions this week and stop what you are doing to 'hurry' to greet someone you don't know.

DAY 04   Look up verse 5 in the King James or New King James version of the Bible. Abraham's offer of a 'morsel' was quite different from what was eventually prepared and served to the guests in verse 6-7. How can his example of delivering more than promised become a workable template for welcoming strangers in your world today?

DAY 05   Revisit the back half of the passage for this week starting at verse 9. In your journal, relate what you read to the New Testament instruction you find in Hebrews 13:2.

BE WELCOMED IN THIS PLACE

THERE'S JUST NOT ENOUGH

——

1 KINGS 17:1-16

[1] Now Elijah the Tishbite, from Tishbe in Gilead, said to Ahab, "As the LORD, the God of Israel, lives, whom I serve, there will be neither dew nor rain in the next few years except at my word." [2] Then the word of the LORD came to Elijah: [3] "Leave here, turn eastward and hide in the Kerith Ravine, east of the Jordan. [4] You will drink from the brook, and I have directed the ravens to supply you with food there." [5] So he did what the LORD had told him. He went to the Kerith Ravine, east of the Jordan, and stayed there. [6] The ravens brought him bread and meat in the morning and bread and meat in the evening, and he drank from the brook. [7] Some time later the brook dried up because there had been no rain in the land. [8] Then the word of the LORD came to him: [9] "Go at once to Zarephath in the region of Sidon and stay there. I have directed a widow there to supply you with food." [10] So he went to Zarephath. When he came to the town gate, a widow was there gathering sticks. He called to her and asked, "Would you bring me a little water in a jar so I may have a drink?" [11] As she was going to get it, he called, "And bring me, please, a piece of bread." [12] "As surely as the LORD your God lives," she replied, "I don't have any bread—only a handful of flour in a jar and a little olive oil in a jug. I am gathering a few sticks to take home and make a meal for myself and my son, that we may eat it—and die." [13] Elijah said to her, "Don't be afraid. Go home and do as you have said. But first make a small loaf of bread for me from what you have and bring it to me, and then make something for yourself and your son. [14] For this is what the LORD, the God of Israel, says: 'The jar of flour will not be used up and the jug of oil will not run dry until the day the LORD sends rain on the land.'" [15] She went away and did as Elijah had told her. So there was food every day for Elijah and for the woman and her family. [16] For the jar of flour was not used up and the jug of oil did not run dry, in keeping with the word of the LORD spoken by Elijah.

SESSION QUESTIONS

—

WEEK SIX

DAY 01

Often we want to wait until we have "enough" before we are willing to be generous with our time, talents, possessions, and our very selves. But most of the time, our view of "enough" morphs and changes according to our situation in a way that makes it easy to spend "surplus" on ourselves. Which one of us has not found something to spend additional money on, filled our extra time with some needless activity, or put off reaching out till we thought we had enough spiritual health or knowledge? Meet the widow in 1 Kings 17:1-16. If ever there was someone who could use the excuse of not having enough for turning a stranger away, it was her. Write down what you learn from her generosity toward Elijah.

DAY 02

The widow from I Kings 17 lived in a pagan land and would only have knowledge of God and His prophets from rumors and stories. Read through the passage again, focusing in on verse 13. Notice that the stranger (Elijah) asked her to make his food first and then prepare a meal for herself and son. Think about how the actions of the widow embody Philippians 2:1-4? How can you live more like this at work, school, home, etc?

DAY 03

Let's meet another woman whose brief story is recorded in Luke 21:1-4 & Mark 12:41-44. Notice the word "all." Find this word in Deut. 6:5. Knowing that the primary way we serve God is by serving others, make some notes about how you can mimic the offering of this widow in ways that include more than just money.

DAY 04

Look up John 12:1-10. Pay attention to the amount of perfume Mary used. It would have been tempting to hold back some of it for herself or sell it like Judas suggested. Why do you think she greeted Jesus in such an extravagant way? How can your relationship with Him be the motivation for extravagance toward others? Like yesterday's exercise, think beyond money and possessions. How could your love for Jesus be shown to others through extravagant love, mercy, forgiveness or compassion as well?

DAY 05

Consider the stories of the three women that you read this week. Each of them could have held back what little they had out of fear or self-preservation, but chose to give. Instead of becoming impoverished by their gifts as we might have expected, they were each greatly enriched through generosity! Jesus' words in Luke 6:38 apply far beyond finances. Spend some time praying over this verse, asking God to show you how you can with an open hand, and an open heart, give generously to others.

BE WELCOMED IN THIS PLACE

SO YOU DON'T LIKE TO COOK...

—

1 PETER 4:7-11

[7] The end of all things is near. Therefore be alert and of sober mind so that you may pray. [8] Above all, love each other deeply, because love covers over a multitude of sins. [9] Offer hospitality to one another without grumbling. [10] Each of you should use whatever gift you have received to serve others, as faithful stewards of God's grace in its various forms.

[11] If anyone speaks, they should do so as one who speaks the very words of God. If anyone serves, they should do so with the strength God provides, so that in all things God may be praised through Jesus Christ. To him be the glory and the power for ever and ever. Amen.

SESSION QUESTIONS

———

WEEK SEVEN

DAY 01 Begin by reading through the passage of Scripture for this week. Then, go back and reread the first sentence. Hospitality doesn't seem to fit into the pressing declaration that the end of time is at hand. Why do you think Peter included it in this section of his letter? Does that give more weight and urgency to the value of showing hospitality to others? Journal your thoughts.

DAY 02 Let's be honest. Even though we have spent several weeks learning about different aspects of hospitality, the tendency is still to equate it primarily with dinner parties and hosting. For some people, that type of hospitality comes naturally, but what if you just don't like big parties, don't have sufficient space, or aren't really into Pinterest? How can what you read in verses 10 & 11 encourage you to explore different ways to serve and welcome others in the name of Jesus?

DAY 03 Add 1 Cor. 12:4-11 to what you have read so far this week. Study verse 7 to see who has spiritual gifts, where they come from, and the purpose for which they are given. Reread 1 Peter 4:10-11 for more insight into why gifts of the Spirit are given.

DAY 04 You have a gift. Do you know which spiritual gift God has given you? Begin to pray and think about how you can use this ability to fulfill the instruction of 1 Peter 4:9.

DAY 05 Start reading verse 11 at "so that." While you are serving others, the real goal is to bring praise to Jesus. Remind yourself of His exalted position by reading Rev. 1:12-18; 5:1-14; 19:1-16; 22:1-21. End your week by adding your voice to the live version of Chris Tomlin's song, How Great is Our God.

BE WELCOMED IN THIS PLACE

BEYOND THE DINNER TABLE

—

LUKE 10:25-37

[25] On one occasion an expert in the law stood up to test Jesus. "Teacher," he asked, "what must I do to inherit eternal life?" [26] "What is written in the Law?" he replied. "How do you read it?" [27] He answered, "'Love the Lord your God with all your heart and with all your soul and with all your strength and with all your mind'; and, 'Love your neighbor as yourself.'" [28] "You have answered correctly," Jesus replied. "Do this and you will live." [29] But he wanted to justify himself, so he asked Jesus, "And who is my neighbor?" [30] In reply Jesus said: "A man was going down from Jerusalem to Jericho, when he was attacked by robbers. They stripped him of his clothes, beat him and went away, leaving him half dead. [31] A priest happened to be going down the same road, and when he saw the man, he passed by on the other side. [32] So too, a Levite, when he came to the place and saw him, passed by on the other side. [33] But a Samaritan, as he traveled, came where the man was; and when he saw him, he took pity on him. [34] He went to him and bandaged his wounds, pouring on oil and wine. Then he put the man on his own donkey, brought him to an inn and took care of him. [35] The next day he took out two denarii and gave them to the innkeeper. 'Look after him,' he said, 'and when I return, I will reimburse you for any extra expense you may have.' [36] "Which of these three do you think was a neighbor to the man who fell into the hands of robbers?" [37] The expert in the law replied, "The one who had mercy on him." Jesus told him, "Go and do likewise."

SESSION QUESTIONS

—

WEEK EIGHT

DAY 01 Many of us enjoy having friends and/or family to our homes. While that's certainly one type of hospitality, biblical hospitality asks that we go beyond what's comfortable and reach out to those who are unfamiliar and may be quite different from us. Before you read Luke 10:25-37, Google about the history of the animosity that existed between the Samaritans and the Jews. How does knowing the background change your understanding of the story in Luke? If you were to "go and do likewise," to whom would you need to reach out? Be specific.

DAY 02 Have you ever been moved by the condition of the poor, sick, handicapped, or elderly? What do you do about those feelings? Read Psalm 82:3-4 and James 1:27. Write down ways you can begin to treat all people as your "neighbors."

DAY 03 Doing life with people is messy. They can disappoint us, stiffen with resistance, may reject genuine compassion, and can even lash out in anger, but as believers, we're called to love. Read what Jesus said in Luke 6:27-36 about another group who we're less likely to feel hospitable toward. Write down a few people you need to "bless" and "pray for" that you haven't before. (Think about an unreasonable boss, self-important co-worker, annoying neighbor, etc) In prayer, ask God to soften your heart toward this group and help you to begin to show deliberate kindness to them.

DAY 04 Find Eph. 2:10 in the Amplified Bible translation. Note how it describes you. Consider all the creations of God in the universe… from the smallest flower in the forest to the most enormous stars in the galaxy. Yet He designates you as His "master work"! Reflect on this thought for a few minutes. Then, look at the end of verse 10 to see why He created you as He did.

DAY 05 Review the people to whom we're called to show hospitality that you read about this week. Then, return to Matt 25:31-46 (from week 2). Focus in on verses 37-40. Who are "the least of these" in your world? Connect this passage to yesterday's verse, realizing that taking care of these people isn't being nice or fulfilling civic-minded duty, but according to Ephesians 2:10, it's part of the work that has been prepared by God for you. What "good works" can you do not only for them, but for God?

BE WELCOMED IN THIS PLACE

TOGETHER FOR THE TRUTH

—

3 JOHN

[1] The elder, To my dear friend Gaius, whom I love in the truth. [2] Dear friend I pray that you may enjoy good health and that all may go well with you, even as your soul is getting along well. [3] It gave me great joy when some believers came and testified about your faithfulness to the truth, telling how you continue to walk in it. [4] I have no greater joy than to hear that my children are walking in the truth. [5] Dear friend, you are faithful in what you are doing for the brothers and sisters, even though they are strangers to you. [6] They have told the church about your love. Please send them on their way in a manner that honors God. [7] It was for the sake of the Name that they went out, receiving no help from the pagans. [8] We ought therefore to show hospitality to such people so that we may work together for the truth.

[9] I wrote to the church, but Diotrephes, who loves to be first, will not welcome us. [10] So when I come, I will call attention to what he is doing, spreading malicious nonsense about us. Not satisfied with that, he even refuses to welcome other believers. He also stops those who want to do so and puts them out of the church. [11] Dear friend, do not imitate what is evil but what is good. Anyone who does what is good is from God. Anyone who does what is evil has not seen God. [12] Demetrius is well spoken of by everyone—and even by the truth itself. We also speak well of him, and you know that our testimony is true. [13] I have much to write you, but I do not want to do so with pen and ink. [14] I hope to see you soon, and we will talk face to face. Peace to you. The friends here send their greetings. Greet the friends there by name.

SESSION QUESTIONS

—

WEEK NINE

DAY 01   Third John introduces two men: Gaius (to whom the letter is written) and Diotrephes. Compare what John said about them and write down anything you learn about hospitality from their example.

DAY 02   Go back through verse 1-8 to see how Gaius treated strangers. Look up Lev. 19:33-34. What reason does the Law give for welcoming strangers? How can your change in status from "alien" to "resident" in the kingdom of God also motivate a change in your attitude toward others? Apply these verses to how you treat those who would normally be considered outsiders to your world.

DAY 03   The commendation that John gives Gaius is specifically related to how he treated strangers in the church. Focus in on vs 6-8 and read Hebrews 13:1-3. How can your hospitality to other Christians whom you don't know very well help us all "work together for the truth?"

DAY 04   Today look at Diotrephes in 3 John 9-11. Write down a list of attitudes and actions in his character that lead to division and discord in the church. (Include other root issues that he may have had, like pride, prejudice, critical spirit, etc.) Are you in a place of leadership at church, community or workplace? How can you guard against these attitudes and create a space that is welcoming to even the people you may disagree with?

DAY 05   Flip back through the entire 8-week session. How has your understanding of hospitality changed? What impacted you the most? Remind yourself that hospitality is at its core an attribute of God and a picture of grace. Close this session by reading through Eph. 2:5-22 again. Offer thanks for the welcoming heart of God and respond by giving yourself to Him to be an instrument of His grace.

VI

STRONG & COURAGEOUS

VI

SESSION SIX

"Hang in there. You can do it!" How many times have you heard that? Maybe someone said it to "encourage" you when you were facing an exceptionally tough situation. Or maybe it was you who said it hoping to "bless" someone else. That kind of statement is usually intended as positive inspiration to push us forward so that we won't give up... a kind of "one size fits all" affirmation that says if we just dig in with all our might and refuse to quit, we can overcome whatever we're facing. But is that really the right sort of thing for believers to say, or even believe? Can we rally ourselves enough to eventually "do" whatever "it" is?

If we know anything from life, it's that there are some things that we clearly can NOT do. We don't have the strength, know-how, expertise or experience to get the task done on our own. And even if we have all the necessary skills, we don't always have all the information or details to always bring our situations together in the right way or on what appears to be the proper schedule.

That was definitely Joshua's situation. Most of us have heard about his battle at Jericho, but that's only the most famous of the dozens of kingdoms that he was commanded to conquer across the Jordan River in the Promised Land with only an ill-trained band of former desert dwellers. It was an impossible scenario that seemed doomed to failure, that is, except for one key factor – the faithfulness of God.

When God commissioned Joshua for this assignment, He never once spoke about the talent, power or accomplishments of Joshua. The Lord didn't give him good marks in leadership on his last annual review or nominate him for best warrior status. While Israel's new leader was clearly directed to be "strong and courageous," (Jos. 1:6-9) he wasn't supposed to muster up that determination from within himself. God prefaced this daunting command with a promise of His strength and His unending presence. He said, "As I was with Moses, so I will be with you; I will never leave you nor forsake you." (Jos. 1:5)

In the New Testament, Jesus made that assurance more personal when He sent the Holy Spirit to live in His followers. He says in John 14:16-17, "I will ask the Father, and He will give you another Helper, that He may be with you forever; that is the Spirit of truth … He abides with you and will be in you."

Today, even when we know that we are in God's will, doing what He commands, we may still face what seem to be impossible situations. In those times, we must believe and trust that God is with us (Jos. 1:5), God is in us (Jn 14:17) and God is for us (Rom. 8:31)! Because we have limited sight and often stunted perspective, things may not always turn out the way we intend. We may even be stunned by apparent failure or overwhelmed by what seems to be defeat, but as believers in Christ, God's faithfulness is our promise too. We can confidently know that we are never, never, never alone!

In this final session of our FLOURISH journey, we'll take a look at the entire book of Joshua and begin to build in our hearts a solid and unwavering assurance to know that whatever comes our way, we can keep going and don't have to give up. We can move forward in victory, persevere and endure knowing that even when our strength and ability fails, His never will.

SESSION GOALS

SESSION SIX

STRONG & COURAGEOUS

GOALS

- To put our past mistakes behind and embrace a new future in the freedom God has provided through Jesus.

- To help us see all the experiences of our lives as preparation for God's call to serve Him.

- To guide us in developing a life-long pursuit of God.

- To learn to listen to and rely on the Holy Spirit as we face new (and seemingly impossible) tasks in the future.

- To trace God's caretaking hand in our past as an encouraging reminder of His presence and provision in our future.

QUESTIONS

- The world often encourages women to be 'strong and courageous'. How is the message of the world different from God's call toward strength and courage?

- In what area of your life do you find it most difficult to rely on God? Why?

- Recall a time when you lacked strength and courage. How did you get through it?

- What would you do differently now than you did then?

- What can you do now to prepare for the next big obstacle?

STRONG & COURAGEOUS

MOSES IS DEAD, NOW WHAT?

—

JOSHUA 1

Have you ever wished for a new beginning? That certainly was the case for the Israelites at the outset of the book of Joshua. They had been in the desert for a long time. A journey which should have taken as little as a few weeks lasted for 40 years! But this delay wasn't because someone refused to stop for directions. The entire nation was stalled in the desert because of their own disobedience and lack of faith. (Num. 14) The added consequence of their disbelief was that most who were alive at the time the Hebrews left Egypt were never allowed to set foot in the Promised Land. (14:23) So, by the time we get to Joshua 1, an entire generation of people had died and those who had grown up behind them were tired of wandering and no doubt, ready to move on. It was time for the past to be put in the past… and to begin again. While it was probably exciting to anticipate new opportunities ahead of them, it certainly had to be a little scary as well. This week we'll look at God's preparation of Joshua and the plan to use him to start a new chapter in the life of Israel. At the same time, we'll be challenged to put our past mistakes behind us and follow boldly as God leads us into new phases of life.

[1] After the death of Moses the servant of the LORD, the LORD said to Joshua son of Nun, Moses' aide: [2] "Moses my servant is dead. Now then, you and all these people, get ready to cross the Jordan River into the land I am about to give to them—to the Israelites. [3] I will give you every place where you set your foot, as I promised Moses. [4] Your territory will extend from the desert to Lebanon, and from the great river, the Euphrates—all the Hittite country—to the Mediterranean Sea in the west. [5] No one will be able to stand against you all the days of your life. As I was with Moses, so I will be with you; I will never leave you nor forsake you.

[6] Be strong and courageous, because you will lead these people to inherit the land I swore to their ancestors to give them.

[7] "Be strong and very courageous. Be careful to obey all the law my servant Moses gave you; do not turn from it to the right or to the left, that you may be successful wherever you go. [8] Keep this Book of the Law always on your lips; meditate on it day and night, so that you may be careful to do everything written in it. Then you will be prosperous and successful. [9] Have I not commanded you? Be strong and courageous. Do not be afraid; do not be discouraged, for the LORD your God will be with you wherever you go." [10] So Joshua ordered the officers of the people: [11] "Go through the camp and tell the people, 'Get your provisions ready. Three days from now you will cross the Jordan here to go in and take possession of the land the LORD your God is giving you for your own.'"

[12] But to the Reubenites, the Gadites and the half-tribe of Manasseh, Joshua said, [13] "Remember the command that Moses the servant of the LORD gave you after he said, 'The LORD your God will give you rest by giving you this land.' [14] Your wives, your children and your livestock may stay in the land that Moses gave you east of the Jordan, but all your fighting men, ready for battle, must cross over ahead of your fellow Israelites. You are to help them [15] until the LORD gives them rest, as he has done for you, and until they too have taken possession of the land the LORD your God is giving them. After that, you may go back and occupy your own land, which Moses the servant of the LORD gave you east of the Jordan toward the sunrise." [16] Then they answered Joshua, "Whatever you have commanded us we will do, and wherever you send us we will go. [17] Just as we fully obeyed Moses, so we will obey you. Only may the LORD your God be with you as he was with Moses. [18] Whoever rebels against your word and does not obey it, whatever you may command them, will be put to death. Only be strong and courageous!"

SESSION QUESTIONS

—

WEEK ONE

DAY 01 Read through Joshua 1. How do you think Joshua felt when he heard these words from God? Are you facing a change of some kind? For example, a new job, change in marital status, a health crisis, a blended family. Is there a leadership role you're being asked to consider? How do you feel about the prospects ahead of you? What do you read in this first chapter that will help you step into a new opportunity confidently trusting in Jesus?

DAY 02 Let's get to know Joshua. Read Exodus 17:8-16; 24:13-18; 32:1-17; 33:7-11. Start a list of what you learn about him from these passages. Along with things that are specifically stated, include things that are implied by his actions as well. [Exodus 17:10: Joshua was a warrior (stated) and was courageous (implied). Exodus 17:13: Joshua was a leader (stated) and determined/diligent (implied) etc.]

DAY 03 Continuing the exercise from yesterday, make notes on what you discover about Joshua from Numbers 14:1-38; 27:12-23; Deut. 1:35-39; 31:1-8. From the passages you've read so far this week, can you see how God was grooming him for his eventual position as leader of Israel? In what ways has God been preparing you for service? Don't just think about the good things that have happened to you, review James 1:2-4 to be reminded of the spiritual purpose of trials and difficult times.

DAY 04 Though the Bible doesn't specifically say, it's fair to assume Joshua was born as a slave in Egypt and was one of the millions of Hebrews who were freed by God through Moses in the exodus from captivity. From this humble and obscure background, Joshua was lifted to a key role in the story God was unfolding. Take some time to reflect on your personal history. Instead of allowing negative experiences to continue to hinder you, think how God might use your past and present to prepare you for a yet unknown avenue of service. End this time of reflection by thanking God for His ability to redeem and restore all things (1 Pet 5:10).

DAY 05 Go back to Joshua 1:1-2. Consider Joshua's relationship with Moses. Though he was now off the scene, notice how God continued to refer to Israel's greatest leader all the way through verse 7. Consider your relationship with your mentor over the past year and what you've learned about Jesus from her. How might her influence live on in you in the years to come? And could there be a spiritual parallel between this moment in your life and that of Joshua? Begin to pray and seek God… Is He calling you to step into the role of spiritual mentor for others?

RESCUED & REDEEMED

—

JOSHUA 2

STRONG & COURAGEOUS

¹ Then Joshua son of Nun secretly sent two spies from Shittim. "Go, look over the land," he said, "especially Jericho." So they went and entered the house of a prostitute named Rahab and stayed there. ² The king of Jericho was told, "Look, some of the Israelites have come here tonight to spy out the land." ³ So the king of Jericho sent this message to Rahab: "Bring out the men who came to you and entered your house, because they have come to spy out the whole land." ⁴ But the woman had taken the two men and hidden them. She said, "Yes, the men came to me, but I did not know where they had come from. ⁵ At dusk, when it was time to close the

city gate, they left. I don't know which way they went. Go after them quickly. You may catch up with them." [6] (But she had taken them up to the roof and hidden them under the stalks of flax she had laid out on the roof.) [7] So the men set out in pursuit of the spies on the road that leads to the fords of the Jordan, and as soon as the pursuers had gone out, the gate was shut. [8] Before the spies lay down for the night, she went up on the roof [9] and said to them, "I know that the LORD has given you this land and that a great fear of you has fallen on us, so that all who live in this country are melting in fear because of you. [10] We have heard how the LORD dried up the water of the Red Sea for you when you came out of Egypt, and what you did to Sihon and Og, the two kings of the Amorites east of the Jordan, whom you completely destroyed. [11] When we heard of it, our hearts melted in fear and everyone's courage failed because of you, for the LORD your God is God in heaven above and on the earth below.

[12] "Now then, please swear to me by the LORD that you will show kindness to my family, because I have shown kindness to you. Give me a sure sign [13] that you will spare the lives of my father and mother, my brothers and sisters, and all who belong to them—and that you will save us from death." [14] "Our lives for your lives!" the men assured her. "If you don't tell what we are doing, we will treat you kindly and faithfully when the LORD gives us the land." [15] So she let them down by a rope through the window, for the house she lived in was part of the city wall.

[16] She said to them, "Go to the hills so the pursuers will not find you. Hide yourselves there three days until they return, and then go on your way." [17] Now the men had said to her, "This oath you made us swear will not be binding on us [18] unless, when we enter the land, you have tied this scarlet cord in the window through which you let us down, and unless you have brought your father and mother, your brothers and all your family into your house.

[19] If any of them go outside your house into the street, their blood will be on their own heads; we will not be responsible. As for those who are in the house with you, their blood will be on our head if a hand is laid on them [20] But if you tell what we are doing, we will be released from the oath you made us swear."

[21] "Agreed," she replied. "Let it be as you say." So she sent them away, and they departed. And she tied the scarlet cord in the window. [22] When they left, they went into the hills and stayed there three days, until the pursuers had searched all along the road and returned without finding them. [23] Then the two men started back. They went down out of the hills, forded the river and came to Joshua son of Nun and told him everything that had happened to them. [24] They said to Joshua, "The LORD has surely given the whole land into our hands; all the people are melting in fear because of us."

SESSION QUESTIONS

—

WEEK TWO

DAY 01 The story of Rahab and the spies is a familiar one to many people, but sometimes we can know the facts and miss the meaning. Read through Joshua 2. Jot down a few things you learn about Rahab. In just a couple of sentences, make some notes about how you are inspired by this story.

DAY 02 Rahab hid the scouts of the invading army and protected them from the leaders of her own people. How is this an atypical response for someone in Rahab's position? Read through the chapter again to look for the motivation behind her actions. How are her attitudes/actions different from people who cry out to God only when they want Him to save them in a crisis?

DAY 03 Based on culture and religion, Rahab had no chance with God. She was a prostitute ... a "professional" sinner who was immersed in immorality. She lived in a pagan culture which, at the time, had no prophet, no teacher and no access to the Law of God. But none of that mattered to Him. He looked beyond all the apparent obstacles, saw her heart and gave her enough truth to transform her life. Think about the "obstacles" that tried to block your faith journey. How does her story and yours exemplify Isaiah 43:18-19? Read a little more of this chapter with your story in mind. Close by thanking God for pursuing you even when you weren't interested in Him.

DAY 04 Jump forward to Joshua 6:22-25 to see more of Rahab's story after the fall of Jericho. Then go carefully through the genealogy in Matthew 1. Look for her name in verse 5. Who was her son (and daughter-in-law)? Her great grandson? Note the other significant people who are her descendants in the verses that follow (esp. vs 16). In this list of names we can see that God didn't just save Rahab; He included her! Reflect on this idea for a few minutes. Then, consider how her story is also your story!! Jesus includes you! Read Galatians 3:26-4:7 to be reminded of your full adoption into God's family.

DAY 05 Look up Psalm 145:1-7. It's obvious what Rahab would have said if she were to "tell of God's mighty acts," but what would you say? If you were called on to proclaim God's "great deeds" to the next "generation", what story would you tell? This could be your salvation story or some other account of deliverance or restoration. Write it down in your journal.

Read Joshua 3, 4, & 5 before next week.

STRONG & COURAGEOUS

LET THE WALLS COME DOWN

—

JOSHUA 6

[1] Now the gates of Jericho were securely barred because of the Israelites. No one went out and no one came in. [2] Then the LORD said to Joshua, "See, I have delivered Jericho into your hands, along with its king and its fighting men. [3] March around the city once with all the armed men. Do this for six days. [4] Have seven priests carry trumpets of rams' horns in front of the ark. On the seventh day, march around the city seven times, with the priests blowing the trumpets. [5] When you hear them sound a long blast on the trumpets, have the whole army give a loud shout; then the wall of the city will collapse and the army will go up, everyone straight in." [6] So Joshua son of Nun called the priests and said to them, "Take up the ark of the covenant of the LORD and have seven priests carry trumpets in front of it." [7] And he ordered the army, "Advance! March around the city, with an armed guard going ahead of the ark of the LORD." [8] When Joshua had spoken to the people, the seven priests carrying the seven trumpets before the LORD went forward, blowing their trumpets, and the ark of the LORD's covenant followed them. [9] The armed guard marched ahead

of the priests who blew the trumpets, and the rear guard followed the ark. All this time the trumpets were sounding. [10] But Joshua had commanded the army, "Do not give a war cry, do not raise your voices, do not say a word until the day I tell you to shout. Then shout!" [11] So he had the ark of the LORD carried around the city, circling it once. Then the army returned to camp and spent the night there. [12] Joshua got up early the next morning and the priests took up the ark of the LORD. [13] The seven priests carrying the seven trumpets went forward, marching before the ark of the LORD and blowing the trumpets. The armed men went ahead of them and the rear guard followed the ark of the LORD, while the trumpets kept sounding. [14] So on the second day they marched around the city once and returned to the camp. They did this for six days. [15] On the seventh day, they got up at daybreak and marched around the city seven times in the same manner, except that on that day they circled the city seven times. [16] The seventh time around, when the priests sounded the trumpet blast, Joshua commanded the army, "Shout! For the LORD has given you the city! [17] The city and all that is in it are to be devoted to the LORD. Only Rahab the prostitute and all who are with her in her house shall be spared, because she hid the spies we sent. [18] But keep away from the devoted things, so that you will not bring about your own destruction by taking any of them. Otherwise you will make the camp of Israel liable to destruction and bring trouble on it. [19] All the silver and gold and the articles of bronze and iron are sacred to the LORD and must go into his treasury." [20] When the trumpets sounded, the army shouted, and at the sound of the trumpet, when the men gave a loud shout, the wall collapsed; so everyone charged straight in, and they took the city. [21] They devoted the city to the LORD and destroyed with the sword every living thing in it—men and women, young and old, cattle, sheep and donkeys. [22] Joshua said to the two men who had spied out the land, "Go into the prostitute's house and bring her out and all who belong to her, in accordance with your oath to her." [23] So the young men who had done the spying went in and brought out Rahab, her father and mother, her brothers and sisters and all who belonged to her. They brought out her entire family and put them in a place outside the camp of Israel. [24] Then they burned the whole city and everything in it, but they put the silver and gold and the articles of bronze and iron into the treasury of the LORD's house. [25] But Joshua spared Rahab the prostitute, with her family and all who belonged to her, because she hid the men Joshua had sent as spies to Jericho—and she lives among the Israelites to this day. [26] At that time Joshua pronounced this solemn oath: "Cursed before the LORD is the one who undertakes to rebuild this city, Jericho: "At the cost of his firstborn son he will lay its foundations; at the cost of his youngest he will set up its gates." [27] So the LORD was with Joshua, and his fame spread throughout the land.

SESSION QUESTIONS

WEEK THREE

DAY 01

This week we'll spend some time looking at the events surrounding the fall of Jericho, but before we get into the story itself, back up and read the important set up in Joshua 5:13-15. Why is this crucial to what happens in chapter 6? Look for Joshua's attitude of submission (vs 14) and surrender (vs 15). If you are facing a situation that seems as insurmountable as the walls of Jericho, think about how you can position yourself in a similar fashion as Joshua.

DAY 02

Move on to the story in chapter 6. The instructions in verses 1-17 make little sense from a military standpoint. Theorize why God would give a skilled warrior like Joshua such seemingly bizarre orders. Remember that trusting God's plan even when it doesn't seem to make sense is directly related to how well we know Him. Look up the following verses to learn about God's knowledge: Ps 147:5; Is. 46:10-11; Acts 15:16-18; Rom. 11:33-36; 1 John 3:20.

DAY 03

Go back to Joshua 6 and finish reading the chapter. The Israelites were likely astonished by the destruction of the walls of Jericho, but based on what their forefathers had told them about the Exodus and what they'd experienced personally in the desert, God's intervention and power shouldn't have been unexpected. What have you learned from other believers and your own personal experience that will help you when you face great obstacles? Write these down. Read more about God's infinite power in Job 42:2; Ps. 33:6-9; Heb. 1:3; Jer. 32:17; Matt. 19:26.

DAY 04

Reread Joshua 6:17-21 to see the specific instructions given to the Israelites concerning the plunder in Jericho. Then, go through chapter 7 to see what happened as a result of disobedience. Achan failed to realize that "nothing in all creation is hidden from God's sight" (Heb. 4:13). Continue learning about God's presence by reading 1 Kings 8:27; Ps. 90:1-2; 139:7-10; Jer. 23:23-24. Spend some time reflecting on the attributes of God you have studied this week and how they can strengthen your faith when you face "high walls" and "strong fortresses."

DAY 05

Look at what happened in the Valley of Achor (literally: Valley of "Trouble") at the end of Joshua 7:20-26. Flip over to Hosea 2:14-15 to see how this valley makes another appearance in Scripture centuries later. Are you (or have you been) in the Valley of Trouble due to your own decisions or as the result of another person's actions? The hope of the Gospel is that Jesus Christ comes to you and "speaks tenderly" promising to change the place of death, anger and defeat into a place of life and hope. End this week by celebrating the power of Jesus by listening to "Salvation's Tide" (Passion 2016) by Kristian Stanfill.

Read Joshua 8.

SEEING IS BELIEVING?

—

JOSHUA 9

STRONG & COURAGEOUS

[1] Now when all the kings west of the Jordan heard about these things—the kings in the hill country, in the western foothills, and along the entire coast of the Mediterranean Sea as far as Lebanon (the kings of the Hittites, Amorites, Canaanites, Perizzites, Hivites and Jebusites)—[2] they came together to wage war against Joshua and Israel.

[3] However, when the people of Gibeon heard what Joshua had done to Jericho and Ai, [4] they resorted to a ruse: They went as a delegation whose donkeys were loaded with worn-out sacks and old wineskins, cracked and mended. [5] They put worn and patched sandals on their feet and wore old clothes. All the bread of their food supply was dry and moldy. [6] Then they went to Joshua in the camp at Gilgal and

said to him and the Israelites, "We have come from a distant country; make a treaty with us." [7] The Israelites said to the Hivites, "But perhaps you live near us, so how can we make a treaty with you?" [8] "We are your servants," they said to Joshua. But Joshua asked, "Who are you and where do you come from?" [9] They answered: "Your servants have come from a very distant country because of the fame of the LORD your God. For we have heard reports of him: all that he did in Egypt,[10] and all that he did to the two kings of the Amorites east of the Jordan—Sihon king of Heshbon, and Og king of Bashan,who reigned in Ashtaroth. [11] And our elders and all those living in our country said to us, 'Take provisions for your journey; go and meet them and say to them, "We are your servants; make a treaty with us."' [12] This bread of ours was warm when we packed it at home on the day we left to come to you. But now see how dry and moldy it is. [13] And these wineskins that we filled were new, but see how cracked they are. And our clothes and sandals are worn out by the very long journey." [14] The Israelites sampled their provisions but did not inquire of the LORD. [15] Then Joshua made a treaty of peace with them to let them live, and the leaders of the assembly ratified it by oath. [16] Three days after they made the treaty with the Gibeonites, the Israelites heard that they were neighbors, living near them. [17] So the Israelites set out and on the third day came to their cities: Gibeon, Kephirah, Beeroth and Kiriath Jearim.

[18] But the Israelites did not attack them, because the leaders of the assembly had sworn an oath to them by the LORD, the God of Israel. The whole assembly grumbled against the leaders, [19] but all the leaders answered, "We have given them our oath by the LORD, the God of Israel, and we cannot touch them now. [20] This is what we will do to them: We will let them live, so that God's wrath will not fall on us for breaking the oath we swore to them." [21] They continued, "Let them live, but let them be woodcutters and water carriers in the service of the whole assembly." So the leaders' promise to them was kept.[22] Then Joshua summoned the Gibeonites and said, "Why did you deceive us by saying, 'We live a long way from you,' while actually you live near us? [23] You are now under a curse: You will never be released from service as woodcutters and water carriers for the house of my God." [24] They answered Joshua, "Your servants were clearly told how the LORD your God had commanded his servant Moses to give you the whole land and to wipe out all its inhabitants from before you. So we feared for our lives because of you, and that is why we did this. [25] We are now in your hands. Do to us whatever seems good and right to you." [26] So Joshua saved them from the Israelites, and they did not kill them. [27] That day he made the Gibeonites woodcutters and water carriers for the assembly, to provide for the needs of the altar of the LORD at the place the LORD would choose. And that is what they are to this day.

SESSION QUESTIONS

—

WEEK FOUR

DAY 01 The story in Joshua 9 may not be as familiar as some of the other parts of this book. Read through the first 8 verses, noting the 2 different attack strategies the people in Canaan used against Israel (vs 1-2 and 3-4). In the world today, we face attacks both externally (from those who try to inflict physical, financial or other direct harm) and internally (from those who try to inflict mental, emotional or more indirect harm). Which is more effective on you? Why? Realizing this, how can you begin to build a defense against this type of strategy?

DAY 02 Read all of Joshua 9. With the omniscient God on the Israelite's side, it seems like the deception of the Gibeonites would have been discovered quickly. Go back to verse 14 to see Joshua's critical mistake. Have you ever made this same kind of error? That is, you trusted what you saw, heard, tasted and touched more than trusting God to guide you? What was the outcome?

DAY 03 Once the dishonesty was discovered, it seems like it might have been OK to ignore the treaty since the Israelites were deceived into making it, but that's not what happened. Go back to Joshua 9 and pick up reading at verse 14. Once you understand why they didn't destroy the people from Gibeon (vs 18), what good leadership qualities do you see in Joshua in the way he handled this situation? Is there anything you can emulate from his example?

DAY 04 Look up 2 Corinthians 6:14-18. How does what you read apply to the story you read this week in Joshua? These verses are frequently applied to marriage, and while that's certainly one application, think about how they might also apply to any kind of oath or contract made between believers and unbelievers.

DAY 05 Take some time to read and reflect on these passages about God's promise to guide you. Psalm 25:8-14; 32:8-11; 73:22-26; 119:97-105; Is. 48:16-17; 58:11; Matt. 7:7-11. Coupled with the verses on His character from last week, scripture reveals our God as all powerful, all knowing, present in all situations and willing to guide His children in all cases. What concrete steps can you implement that will help you learn to trust Jesus more than you trust yourself?

Read Joshua 10

TAKING THE LAND

—

JOSHUA 11

STRONG & COURAGEOUS

[1] When Jabin king of Hazor heard of this, he sent word to Jobab king of Madon, to the kings of Shimron and Akshaph, [2] and to the northern kings who were in the mountains, in the Arabah south of Kinnereth, in the western foothills and in Naphoth Dor on the west; [3] to the Canaanites in the east and west; to the Amorites, Hittites, Perizzites and Jebusites in the hill country; and to the Hivites below Hermon in the region of Mizpah. [4] They came out with all their troops and a large number of horses and chariots—a huge army, as numerous as the sand on the seashore. [5] All these kings joined forces and made camp together at the Waters of Merom to fight against Israel. [6] The LORD said to Joshua, "Do not be afraid of them, because by this time tomorrow I will hand all of them, slain, over to Israel. You are to hamstring their horses and burn their chariots." [7] So Joshua and his whole army came against them suddenly at the Waters of Merom and attacked them, [8] and the LORD gave them into the hand of Israel. They defeated them and pursued them all the way to Greater Sidon, to Misrephoth Maim, and to the Valley of Mizpah on the east, until no survivors were left. [9] Joshua did to them as the LORD had directed: He hamstrung their horses and burned their chariots.

[10] At that time Joshua turned back and captured Hazor and put its king to the sword. (Hazor had been the head of all these kingdoms.) [11] Everyone in it they

put to the sword. They totally destroyed them, not sparing anyone that breathed, and he burned Hazor itself. [12] Joshua took all these royal cities and their kings and put them to the sword. He totally destroyed them, as Moses the servant of the LORD had commanded. [13] Yet Israel did not burn any of the cities built on their mounds—except Hazor, which Joshua burned. [14] The Israelites carried off for themselves all the plunder and livestock of these cities, but all the people they put to the sword until they completely destroyed them, not sparing anyone that breathed. [15] As the LORD commanded his servant Moses, so Moses commanded Joshua, and Joshua did it; he left nothing undone of all that the LORD commanded Moses. [16] So Joshua took this entire land: the hill country, all the Negev, the whole region of Goshen, the western foothills, the Arabah and the mountains of Israel with their foothills, [17] from Mount Halak, which rises toward Seir, to Baal Gad in the Valley of Lebanon below Mount Hermon. He captured all their kings and put them to death. [18] Joshua waged war against all these kings for a long time. [19] Except for the Hivites living in Gibeon, not one city made a treaty of peace with the Israelites, who took them all in battle. [20] For it was the LORD himself who hardened their hearts to wage war against Israel, so that he might destroy them totally, exterminating them without mercy, as the LORD had commanded Moses. [21] At that time Joshua went and destroyed the Anakites from the hill country: from Hebron, Debir and Anab, from all the hill country of Judah, and from all the hill country of Israel. Joshua totally destroyed them and their towns. [22] No Anakites were left in Israelite territory; only in Gaza, Gath and Ashdod did any survive. [23] So Joshua took the entire land, just as the LORD had directed Moses, and he gave it as an inheritance to Israel according to their tribal divisions. Then the land had rest from war.

The middle and latter half of Joshua contains the kinds of passages that are tempting to skim over lightly or skip all together to move on to something more "exciting", but remember that "all Scripture is God-breathed and is useful for teaching, rebuking, correcting and training in righteousness" (2 Tim 3:16). That means that we can find application for things we face today in every inch of the Word. It can take a little longer and require a little more thought, but when we prayerfully read and take time to listen to the Spirit, Truth will begin to jump off the pages. Before you read Joshua 11, back up and get the context for the events by looking at Joshua 10:40-43. If you haven't read all of chapter 10, do so now to see an amazing miracle God performed on behalf of Israel .

SESSION QUESTIONS

—

WEEK FIVE

DAY 01 By the time chapter 10 closes, all of the kings in the southern part of Canaan had been subdued, but chapter 11 reveals a new threat. After hearing about the Israelite conquest, the Northern empires centralized under one king and mounted an offensive that was much larger, better equipped and organized than any of Israel's previous enemies. Read verses 1-6. What made Joshua confident even when facing overwhelming odds? Trust in God's faithfulness is the source of our confidence too. Look up Deut. 7:8-9; 1 Kings 8:56-61; Ps. 9:7-10; 33:4-5; Lam 3:22-23; 2 Thess. 3:3; Heb. 10:19-23. Write down how these verses can help you when you feel outnumbered.

DAY 02 Continue reading Joshua 11:6-12. Horses and chariots would seem like useful tools to incorporate into the arsenal of Israel in order to give them an advantage as they took and held the Promised Land. Why do you think God gave Joshua the instructions that He did at the end of verse 6? Look up Psalm 20 and Isaiah 31:1-3 for some help. What does that tell you about relying on modern ideas, strategies, or tactics when you face difficult situations?

DAY 03 Keep reading through verse 15 in Joshua 11. Look at the words "nothing" and "all" in the last verse you read today. As you reflect on the thoroughness of Joshua's obedience to God's commands, is there an area of your personal, ethical, or moral life where you need to adopt Joshua's attitude? Is there follow-through that needs to take place so that you can also do "all" that God commands? Bring these issues to Jesus in prayer. Invite the Spirit to reveal anything that keeps you from moving into full obedience.

DAY 04 Up till this point, God intervened in miraculous ways to defeat the inhabitants of Canaan, but in this chapter, there are no stories like that. How could the Israelites be confident that God was still with them? See Num. 23:19; Heb. 13:8; James 1:17. What encouragement and assurance can you draw from this that will see you through the times when God seems inactive or silent?

DAY 05 Chapter 12 is a summary of the defeat of the kingdoms (and kings) in Canaan (vs 9-24). If you were to give names to the "kings" that have tried to block you from possessing what has been given by Jesus and now rightfully belongs to you, what would they be? (ex. The King of Inferiority, The King of Materialism, The King of Abuse, The King of Anger, etc.) Write these in your journal and over the top, copy 1 Corinthians 15:57.

Read Joshua 12.

STRONG & COURAGEOUS

REST ASSURED

—

JOSHUA 13

[1] When Joshua had grown old, the LORD said to him, "You are now very old, and there are still very large areas of land to be taken over. [2] "This is the land that remains: all the regions of the Philistines and Geshurites, [3] from the Shihor River on the east of Egypt to the territory of Ekron on the north, all of it counted as Canaanite though held by the five Philistine rulers in Gaza, Ashdod, Ashkelon, Gath and Ekron; the territory of the Avvites [4] on the south; all the land of the Canaanites, from Arah of the Sidonians as far as Aphek and the border of the Amorites; [5] the area of Byblos; and all Lebanon to the east, from Baal Gad below Mount Hermon to Lebo Hamath. [6] "As for all the inhabitants of the mountain regions from Lebanon to Misrephoth Maim, that is, all the Sidonians, I myself will drive them out before the Israelites. Be sure to allocate this land to Israel for an inheritance, as I have instructed you, [7] and divide it as an inheritance among the nine tribes and half of the tribe of Manasseh." [8] The other half of Manasseh, the Reubenites and the Gadites had received the inheritance that Moses had given them east of the Jordan, as he, the servant of the LORD, had assigned it to them. [9] It extended from Aroer on the rim of the Arnon Gorge, and from the town in the middle of the gorge, and included the whole plateau of Medeba as far as Dibon, [10] and all the towns of Sihon king of the Amorites, who ruled in Heshbon, out to the border of the Ammonites. [11] It also included Gilead, the territory of the people of Geshur and Maakah, all of Mount Hermon and all Bashan as far as Salekah— [12] that is, the whole kingdom of Og in Bashan,who had reigned in Ashtaroth and Edrei. (He was the last of the Rephaites.) Moses had

defeated them and taken over their land. [13] But the Israelites did not drive out the people of Geshur and Maakah, so they continue to live among the Israelites to this day. [14] But to the tribe of Levi he gave no inheritance, since the food offerings presented to the LORD, the God of Israel, are their inheritance, as he promised them. [15] This is what Moses had given to the tribe of Reuben, according to its clans: [16] The territory from Aroer on the rim of the Arnon Gorge, and from the town in the middle of the gorge, and the whole plateau past Medeba [17] to Heshbon and all its towns on the plateau, including Dibon, Bamoth Baal, Beth Baal Meon, [18] Jahaz, Kedemoth, Mephaath, [19] Kiriathaim, Sibmah, Zereth Shahar on the hill in the valley, [20] Beth Peor, the slopes of Pisgah, and Beth Jeshimoth— [21] all the towns on the plateau and the entire realm of Sihon king of the Amorites, who ruled at Heshbon. Moses had defeated him and the Midianite chiefs, Evi, Rekem, Zur, Hur and Reba—princes allied with Sihon—who lived in that country. [22] In addition to those slain in battle, the Israelites had put to the sword Balaam son of Beor, who practiced divination. [23] The boundary of the Reubenites was the bank of the Jordan. These towns and their villages were the inheritance of the Reubenites, according to their clans.

[24] This is what Moses had given to the tribe of Gad, according to its clans: [25] The territory of Jazer, all the towns of Gilead and half the Ammonite country as far as Aroer, near Rabbah; [26] and from Heshbon to Ramath Mizpah and Betonim, and from Mahanaim to the territory of Debir; [27] and in the valley, Beth Haram, Beth Nimrah, Sukkoth and Zaphon with the rest of the realm of Sihon king of Heshbon (the east side of the Jordan, the territory up to the end of the Sea of Galilee). [28] These towns and their villages were the inheritance of the Gadites, according to their clans. [29] This is what Moses had given to the half-tribe of Manasseh, that is, to half the family of the descendants of Manasseh, according to its clans: [30] The territory extending from Mahanaim and including all of Bashan, the entire realm of Og king of Bashan—all the settlements of Jair in Bashan, sixty towns, [31] half of Gilead, and Ashtaroth and Edrei (the royal cities of Og in Bashan). This was for the descendants of Makir son of Manasseh— for half of the sons of Makir, according to their clans. [32] This is the inheritance Moses had given when he was in the plains of Moabacross the Jordan east of Jericho. [33] But to the tribe of Levi, Moses had given no inheritance; the LORD, the God of Israel, is their inheritance, as he promised them.

SESSION QUESTIONS

—

DAY 01

In Joshua 13:1-7, God tells Israel about the battles yet to be fought in Canaan and reminds them that He will go before them to drive out the inhabitants (vs 1:6). From what you know from other known stories of the Old Testament, did Israel follow through on the instructions to fully take the land? Look for a familiar group of people named in vs 2. Read 1 Sam 4:1-10 to learn about one specific incident with this group. Type this name in a Bible search to see how many times it shows up later in Israel's history. When God tells us to drive disobedience and sin completely from our lives, what can we learn about the danger of partial obedience from Israel's mistake?

DAY 02

Joshua 13 chronicles the beginning of dividing the land of Canaan among the tribes of Israel. Focus specifically on the inheritance given to the Levites (vs 14 and 33) who were priests and caretakers of the tabernacle/temple (Num. 1:47-53). Then look up 1 Pet. 2:9-10 to see one of your roles in God's kingdom. According to these passages, what (or who) is your inheritance? As you come around this idea, look up Eph. 1:11-14 and Heb. 9:15. Write down what you think it means for God to be your inheritance. Use the rest of the week to go through chapter 15-19 to see the entire division of the land.

DAY 03

Look back at Joshua 14:15. Then, go to Genesis 15:18-20 to see the beginning of God's declaration about the Promised Land. Compare those verses to Exodus 6:8 and Joshua 1:4. Over 400 years elapsed before the Israelites finally possessed Canaan and, for a time, dwelt in peace. How can this comfort and encourage you when you face long seasons of waiting when it feels like nothing is happening? Look back at the verses from Day 2 of last week for a reminder of God's faithfulness.

DAY 04

Joshua led Israel to take the possession of the land and by the end of chapter 14, the conquest was over and rest came to Israel. Turn over to Hebrews 4 to read a key passage revealing Jesus as our perfect and final rest. Look for Joshua's name in this chapter and make notes about how Jesus provides rest from our futile attempts to attain righteousness before God on our own. End your time in the Word with a prayer of thanksgiving for all that Jesus has done for you.

DAY 05

Look up Matthew 11:25-30. How does this passage give us a deeper understanding of rest? What kind of rest does Jesus provide? How can you possess what has been promised to you by Him?

STRONG & COURAGEOUS

JESUS IN THE CITY

—

JOSHUA 20

[1] Then the LORD said to Joshua: [2] "Tell the Israelites to designate the cities of refuge, as I instructed you through Moses, [3] so that anyone who kills a person accidentally and unintentionally may flee there and find protection from the avenger of blood. [4] When they flee to one of these cities, they are to stand in the entrance of the city gate and state their case before the elders of that city. Then the elders are to admit the fugitive into their city and provide a place to live among them. [5] If the avenger of blood comes in pursuit, the elders must not surrender the fugitive, because the fugitive killed their neighbor unintentionally and without malice aforethought. [6] They are to stay in that city until they have stood trial before the assembly and until the death of the high priest who is serving at that time. Then they may go back to their own home in the town from which they fled." [7] So they set apart Kedesh in Galilee in the hill country of Naphtali, Shechem in the hill country of Ephraim, and Kiriath Arba (that is, Hebron) in the hill country of Judah. [8] East of the Jordan (on the other side from Jericho) they designated Bezer in the wilderness on the plateau in the tribe of Reuben, Ramoth in Gilead in the tribe of Gad, and Golan in Bashan in the tribe of Manasseh.

[9] Any of the Israelites or any foreigner residing among them who killed someone accidentally could flee to these designated cities and not be killed by the avenger of blood prior to standing trial before the assembly.

On a civil level, the Cities of Refuge were established to provide protection for people who unintentionally committed manslaughter. Since this was long before CSI teams, lawyers and rights of due process, retribution was often carried out by the victim's family or a mob well before officials could hear about the incident, hold a trial, and decide on proper punishment according to the Law of Moses. So these six towns were set up to provide an accused person a safe haven from those who sought vengeance. Spiritually speaking, Christ is the City of Refuge for all people. He stands ready to provide protection from the enemy whose intent is to track and hound us until we are destroyed (1 Pet. 5:8). This week we'll take a look at the characteristics of these cities that provide a clear parallel to our relationship with Jesus. As we emulate His love, we can, by our actions and attitudes, extend His offer of shelter to those around us.

SESSION QUESTIONS

DAY 01 Read carefully through Joshua 20. If you Googled the location of the Cities of Refuge on an ancient map, you'd see that they are strategically positioned throughout the Promised Land. This assured that if an accident occurred, the guilty would never be far from a haven of safety. Look up Psalm 17:6-15; 28:6-9 & 73:27-28. Write down how these passages help you relate to Joshua 20.

DAY 02 Once the Cities of Refuge were established, the leaders of Israel were careful to keep the roads clear from debris and overgrowth so that no one would be hindered or lose the path in finding the way to safety. Read Matthew 23. What were the Pharisees doing? What was Jesus' attitude toward their actions? How does the church sometimes do the same thing today? How can you as an individual help smooth out any unintentional blockades that might limit access to the kingdom of God?

DAY 03 Joshua 20:4-6 assured offenders they were secure only within the walls of one these recognized cities. If a wrongdoer ever left the city limits, the person was open to attack and destruction by his enemies. In the spiritual realm, the walls of salvation are our only sure protection from the enemy who seeks our destruction. If a person chooses to live outside a relationship with Jesus, then at the time of judgment, there will be no protection available (Rev. 20:15). Read Acts 4:12 and note where safety is found. Does this give urgency to the command found in Matthew 28:16-20? Write down any action you can take based on this.

DAY 04 Reread Joshua 20:9. Notice that access to the protection in the Cities of Refuge wasn't just open to the Israelites. Move over to Revelation 5:9-10 and 7:9-10 to see that God's mercy is open and available to all. Contemplate the choruses recorded in either of these chapters and end your time in worship for the great gift of salvation that is yours in Jesus!

DAY 05 Review all you've learned this week about the Cities of Refuge and how they foreshadow the work of Jesus on our behalf. Read Romans 10:9-15, specifically thinking about the questions Paul posed in verses 14-15. Begin to ask God how you can be one of those who "brings good news." Keep a record of what He says in response to the offer of your available heart.

Read Joshua 23.

CALLED TO COMMITMENT

—

JOSHUA 24

STRONG & COURAGEOUS

[1] Then Joshua assembled all the tribes of Israel at Shechem. He summoned the elders, leaders, judges and officials of Israel, and they presented themselves before God. [2] Joshua said to all the people, "This is what the LORD, the God of Israel, says: 'Long ago your ancestors, including Terah the father of Abraham and Nahor, lived beyond the Euphrates River and worshiped other gods. [3] But I took your father Abraham from the land beyond the Euphrates and led him throughout Canaan and gave him many descendants. I gave him Isaac, [4] and to Isaac I gave Jacob and Esau. I assigned the hill country of Seir to Esau, but Jacob and his family went down to Egypt. [5] "'Then I sent Moses and Aaron, and I afflicted the Egyptians by what I did there, and I brought you out. [6] When I brought your people out of Egypt, you came to the sea, and the Egyptians pursued them with chariots and horsemen as far as the Red Sea. [7] But they cried to the LORD for help, and he put darkness between you and the Egyptians; he brought the sea over them and covered them. You saw with your own eyes what I did to the Egyptians. Then you lived in the wilderness for a long time. [8] "'I brought you to the land of the Amorites who lived east of the Jordan. They fought against you, but I gave them into your hands. I destroyed them from before you, and you took possession of their land. [9] When Balak son of Zippor, the king of Moab, prepared to fight against Israel, he sent for Balaam son of Beor to put a curse on you. [10] But I would not listen to Balaam, so he blessed you again and again, and I delivered you out of his hand. [11] "'Then you crossed the Jordan and came to Jericho. The citizens of Jericho fought against you, as did also the Amorites, Perizzites, Canaanites, Hittites, Girgashites, Hivites and Jebusites, but I gave them into your hands. [12] I sent the hornet ahead of you, which drove them out before you—also the two Amorite kings. You did not do it with

your own sword and bow. [13] So I gave you a land on which you did not toil and cities you did not build; and you live in them and eat from vineyards and olive groves that you did not plant.' [14] "Now fear the LORD and serve him with all faithfulness. Throw away the gods your ancestors worshiped beyond the Euphrates River and in Egypt, and serve the LORD. [15] But if serving the LORD seems undesirable to you, then choose for yourselves this day whom you will serve, whether the gods your ancestors served beyond the Euphrates, or the gods of the Amorites, in whose land you are living. But as for me and my household, we will serve the LORD." [16] Then the people answered, "Far be it from us to forsake the LORD to serve other gods! [17] It was the LORD our God himself who brought us and our parents up out of Egypt, from that land of slavery, and performed those great signs before our eyes. He protected us on our entire journey and among all the nations through which we traveled. [18] And the LORD drove out before us all the nations, including the Amorites, who lived in the land. We too will serve the LORD, because he is our God."

[19] Joshua said to the people, "You are not able to serve the LORD. He is a holy God; he is a jealous God. He will not forgive your rebellion and your sins. [20] If you forsake the LORD and serve foreign gods, he will turn and bring disaster on you and make an end of you, after he has been good to you."

[21] But the people said to Joshua, "No! We will serve the LORD." [22] Then Joshua said, "You are witnesses against yourselves that you have chosen to serve the LORD."

"Yes, we are witnesses," they replied.

[23] "Now then," said Joshua, "throw away the foreign gods that are among you and yield your hearts to the LORD, the God of Israel." [24] And the people said to Joshua, "We will serve the LORD our God and obey him." [25] On that day Joshua made a covenant for the people, and there at Shechem he reaffirmed for them decrees and laws. [26] And Joshua recorded these things in the Book of the Law of God. Then he took a large stone and set it up there under the oak near the holy place of the LORD.

[27] "See!" he said to all the people. "This stone will be a witness against us. It has heard all the words the LORD has said to us. It will be a witness against you if you are untrue to your God." [28] Then Joshua dismissed the people, each to their own inheritance.

[29] After these things, Joshua son of Nun, the servant of the LORD, died at the age of a hundred and ten. [30] And they buried him in the land of his inheritance, at Timnath Serah in the hill country of Ephraim, north of Mount Gaash. [31] Israel served the LORD throughout the lifetime of Joshua and of the elders who outlived him and who had experienced everything the LORD had done for Israel. [32] And Joseph's bones, which the Israelites had brought up from Egypt, were buried at Shechem in the tract of land that Jacob bought for a hundred pieces of silver from the sons of Hamor, the father of Shechem. This became the inheritance of Joseph's descendants.

[33] And Eleazar son of Aaron died and was buried at Gibeah, which had been allotted to his son Phinehas in the hill country of Ephraim.

SESSION QUESTIONS

—

DAY 01   The last chapter of Joshua begins with a review of the significant events in the life of Israel. Read verses 1-13. What was the point of this history lesson? Spend some time recounting your own history with Jesus. Include how He has worked in the lives of your family and/or other believers who have influenced your walk with Him. How does this exercise strengthen you for the tasks ahead?

DAY 02   Continue reading Joshua 24:14-18. What does it mean to "fear the Lord"? Look up Deut. 10:12-22; Ps. 19:7-11; 119:33-38; Prov. 2:1-5. Write down a concise definition from what you discovered.

DAY 03   Reread the passage in Joshua 24 from yesterday and continue through verse 24. Throwing away idols of their forefathers signified a new undivided devotion to the one true God. Take a survey of your life. What divides your attention and commitment to the Lord? How can you symbolically (or literally) rid yourself from these influences and encourage a steadfast and singular devotion to Jesus?

DAY 04   Go through verses 24-27. At the end of Joshua's challenge to the people, he wrote down their commitment to the Lord and then set up a stone as a reminder of their decision. Is it time for you to "set up a stone" as a reminder of commitments you've made during your time in FLOURISH? Spend some time thanking Jesus for His love, His Word, your mentor, etc. Then, put a reoccurring yearly reminder notification on your phone's calendar to reread Joshua 24 for the purpose of annually assessing your commitment to Jesus.

DAY 05   Finish reading Joshua 24. Think back to when you were just considering being a part of the FLOURISH journey and compare it to where you are now. In the past 12 months, God has called you to growth, richness, and depth of relationship! As you finish out this final session, think about how verse 28 might apply as you metaphorically move out "into your own inheritance." Write down any closing thoughts and end your time with prayer and thanksgiving.

your move

Joshua saw a lot over the span of his long and storied life. He began in Egyptian bondage, and as a young man took his place at Moses' side as God's mighty hand rescued His people out from under the harsh rule of Pharaoh. He saw the Lord part the Red Sea, tasted manna (Ex 16:4) and dressed in clothes that never wore out (Deut. 8:4) as the Israelites wandered in the desert for 40 years. Later, as Moses's successor, he lead the Hebrews through the parted waters of the Jordan River, watched the walls of Jericho crumble, and led the Israelites to conquer their enemies and settle in the Promised Land of Canaan.

And so, it's in that last chapter as he paused to survey the faithfulness and power of God in his life. Joshua gathered the leaders and people together to give them a final challenge.

"Now fear the Lord and serve Him with all faithfulness." ~ Joshua 24:14
Serve Him with ALL faithfulness…

That statement doesn't leave any room for casual faith. It doesn't give the option of following God only when it's convenient or personally beneficial. While the world will never have a shortage of things that distract us and tempt us away from following the Lord's voice, we're continually called to set ourselves apart and invest in serving Him. But this kind of commitment comes from a deeper place than speaking empty words or busying ourselves with religious activity. As you come to the end of this FLOURISH journey of immersing yourself daily in God's Word… of prayer… and of deeper levels of relationship with Jesus, it's significant to take a moment to reflect on Joshua 24:23 once more. In it, Joshua encourages us to "yield (our) hearts to the Lord, the God of Israel."

The easiest way to think about this today is to focus on the thing that's most important: Relationship. And that is, your relationship with Christ. When knowing Him becomes your priority, following and serving the Lord will no longer be obligation, but becomes the overflow of a joyful and grateful heart. We are honored that you have made this journey with us in FLOURISH and celebrate your lives as a testimony of the truth that God's Word does not return empty, but accomplishes all that He desires (Is. 55:11).

As you move into a new chapter in your life, commit yourself to continually pursue Jesus, knowing that perseverance, character and hope are closely intertwined (Rom. 5:3-4). Lean into the Lord and no matter what comes in the years ahead, wholly embrace what He has for you. Invest your lives in others and serve God with all faithfulness. Deliberately open your heart to the Spirit, invite Him to carry on His transforming work, and to equip you for the future He has in store… one that is for your good and His glory!

Heavenly Father,

Help us learn the lesson that Your Word so clearly teaches and with a whole heart, make an undivided commitment to You that will impact our thoughts, attitudes, behaviors and by extension, also impact our families, friends and the world around us. Open our eyes to unrealized areas of compromise and lead us by your Spirit to make any changes that will enable us to more fully honor You. Help us confidently give ourselves fully to you and be willing to step out to serve You whenever, however and wherever You lead. When we are confused by our circumstances and overwhelmed by opposition, remind us of Your past faithfulness and assure us that the work that You began within us will continue until the day we see you face to face (Phil 1:6).

Thank you for all You have done, and will continue to do.
It's in the name of Jesus that we pray.
Amen.

WE'RE WALKING ALONGSIDE

you.

—

We have special training and content for you in your journey as a mentor!

As a team, we want to walk alongside you in this mentoring journey, giving you resources and tips that can make a difference as you navigate these mentoring sessions. Please refer to the next portion of this book to find our Mentor Guidelines, content intended to equip and support you as a mentor.

In addition, you can visit **FlourishMentor.com** for further material, including videos and updated content!

MENTOR GUIDELINES

VISION & GOAL

FLOURISH calls women to a higher standard of living following the commands in Titus 2:3-5—a God-filled life for the sake of the gospel! One where we wholeheartedly love and follow Jesus and aim to view our lives and circumstances through the lens of Scripture: the big story of God.

To become women who flourish, we benefit from the wisdom and encouragement of those who have gone before us and reflect Jesus. We believe a mentoring relationship between women can be rich soil for such growth.

WHY MENTORING?

—

IT'S GOD'S IDEA AND IT GOES BEYOND US.

"But as for you [Titus], teach what accords with sound doctrine. ... Older women likewise are to be reverent in behavior, not slanderers or slaves to much wine. They are to teach what is good, and so train the young women to love their husbands and children, to be self-controlled, pure, working at home, kind, and submissive to their own husbands, that the word of God may not be reviled" (Titus 2:1,3-5, ESV).

Or how The Message version translates it: "Guide older women into lives of reverence so they end up as neither gossips nor drunks, but models of goodness. By looking at them, the younger women will know how to love their husbands and children, be virtuous and pure, keep a good house, be good wives. We don't want anyone looking down on God's Message because of their behavior."

WE MENTOR BECAUSE . . .

▶ We mentor because there is unmistakable evidence in Scripture of the call to mentor the next generation. (See Titus 2; Mal. 4:6; the stories of Elisha and Elijah in 1 and 2 Kings; Isa. 8:18; etc.)

▶ We mentor because the way we live matters, and we are called to influence the way others live as well. We are called to mentor not only because of the quality and the look of our lives, but because of the way we demonstrate God in our lives. We are also called to advance the gospel as Titus 2 describes!

WHY MENTORING?

(continued)

▶ We mentor because these intentional relationships create a safe place for us to listen, ask hard questions, unearth potential, diligently pray for, and unconditionally love the young mentees in our care in all areas of their lives. The goal of this relationship is to point the mentees to Jesus, and He will work out their purposes and places in this world. Mentors serve as a compass always pointing to True North—Jesus.

"So I exhort the elders among you, as a fellow elder and a witness of the sufferings of Christ, as well as a partaker in the glory that is going to be revealed: shepherd the flock of God that is among you, exercising oversight, not under compulsion, but willingly, as God would have you; not for shameful gain, but eagerly; not domineering over those in your charge, but being examples to the flock. And when the chief Shepherd appears, you will receive the unfading crown of glory. Likewise, you who are younger, be subject to the elders. Clothe yourselves, all of you, with humility toward one another, for 'God opposes the proud but gives grace to the humble'" (1 Peter 5:1-5, ESV).

DEFINITION OF MENTORING

▶ Mentors ask questions, help mentees envision goals, and help them achieve goals according to their faith and trust in Jesus.

▶ Mentors provides guidance, not answers.

▶ Guides are people who've traveled a path before, learned along the way, and are willing to assist another traveler. When mentors serve as guides, they show younger travelers the way, offer helpful information, warn of dangers, share their own experiences on the road, and provide first aid if necessary.

▶ Mentoring relationships help push us forward in our faith and challenge us to a higher standard of living in every area of our lives and pursuit of Jesus.

▶ Although mentors don't need to be experts of Scripture, the FLOURISH goal is growth, a higher standard of living encouraged by women who have grown—women who actively produce fruit because of their knowledge of, closeness to, and journey with Jesus.

▶ FLOURISHING happens when women confidently guide women in the path of processing their lives through the lens of Scripture, while loving and pursuing Jesus more.

▶ Jesus is the ultimate model. Christ told us that some of what He taught might not be understood until much later, but He continuously taught with sensitivity and patience (see John 13:7). Jesus took time to answer the disciples' questions (see John 13:6) and used day-to-day dilemmas to illustrate gospel-centered truths.

OUR PURPOSE
AS MENTORS WILL
BE ACCOMPLISHED
AS WE:

- *Value and practice time with Jesus.*
- *Learn to think scripturally about all of life.*
- *Seek to bring our lives under the authority of God's Word.*
- *Apply scriptural principles to relationships and circumstances.*
- *Establish positive relationships.*
- *Desire to mentor other women and pour out what you've received.*
- *Grow in our love for and service to the Church.*
- *Cultivate a life-giving culture in the Church where women share the gospel and share their lives with one another.*
- *Set and achieve specific life goals.*

HOW DO WE MENTOR?

———

FLOURISH is a "show me" journey. The Greek word translated "train" in Titus 2:4 is sophronizo. It carries the idea of helping women cultivate sound judgment by demonstrating or modeling wisdom and discernment for them. It happens when one woman shows another woman the shape of a life with Jesus. Mentoring is relational ministry. Paul captures the essence of mentoring in 1 Thessalonians 2:7-8, "We were gentle among you, like a nursing mother taking care of her own children. So, being affectionately desirous of you, we were ready to share with you not only the gospel of God but also our own selves, because you had become very dear to us" (ESV).[1]

Our main job as mentors is to model a life that glorifies God while praying for and loving our mentees. With the FLOURISH journal, we've provided a devotional foundation for the relationship, but mentoring goes beyond studying Scripture—it's about doing life together and letting the mentees see the fruit you have reaped in your life by following Jesus.

Ideally, the focus of your time with your mentees will be on the practical applications of the themes for each session and not solely the devotional content.

AS MENTORS:

▶ We meet in groups, individually, or both.
▶ We invite mentees into our lives.
▶ We ask a lot of questions and let mentees process their answers.
▶ We keep mentees accountable to their commitment in FLOURISH.
▶ We maintain a delicate balance between accountability and grace.
▶ We confront when necessary.
▶ We are transparent with our own stories and lives, building trust with one another as early as possible in the journey.

[1]*We owe a debt of gratitude to our friend, Susan Hunt, whose insight inspired much of the wisdom in this paragraph.*

YOUR WALK

DAILY WALK

Your own personal walk with Jesus will be reflected in all you do. As you seek Jesus in your own life, you will inspire young women to set intimacy with Christ as a high priority in their own lives. Time with God was a priority for Jesus no matter how busy He was. Your own daily walk needs to be strong so you can point others to Jesus and not to yourself.

Oswald Chambers said, "The lasting value of our public service for God is measured by the depth of the intimacy of our private times of fellowship and oneness with Him."[2] You can only influence others to spend time with Jesus as they see the results of your time spent with God.

DAILY DEPENDENCY

Recognize that your ability to mentor is not based on your talents, your gifts, or even your experiences and success, but on your dependency on living in Christ and dwelling in the Word. He will equip you to do what He's called you to do. It is often in our weakness that God's greatest work is done (see 2 Cor. 12:10). Remember, without Him we can do nothing (see John 15:5); but with Him, we can do all things (see Phil. 4:13).

2. Oswald Chambers, "Worship," My Utmost for His Highest, January 6, https://utmost.org/worship/.

SOME OF THE DO'S

▶ Great mentors listen often— and speak when needed.

▶ Great mentors facilitate by asking open-ended questions and encouraging dialogue.

▶ Great mentors encourage by offering whatever God has given them.

▶ Great mentors advise by coaching others as to how to get answers—rather than by giving answers.

Try to only share from your experiences, what you've done or observed others do firsthand, or from Scripture. You'll never go wrong if you stay within those two guardrails.

▶ Great mentors are present—which is a huge gift!

▶ Great mentors initiate relationship.

▶ Great mentors become loving friends.

SOME OF THE DON'TS

▶ You're <u>not</u> going to be her mom.

▶ You're <u>not</u> going to be her babysitter.

▶ You're <u>not</u> going to be her professional counselor.

▶ You're <u>not</u> going to tell her what to do.

▶ You're <u>not</u> going to project your life on her.

▶ You're <u>not</u> going to fill a void in your life with her.

In summary, your role is to do life with this girl or these girls for a season of time. Be who you are, share what you know, let her see how you think, act, live, pray, and serve. Don't take responsibility for "changing" her. Leave that to Jesus. Just show up and be you.

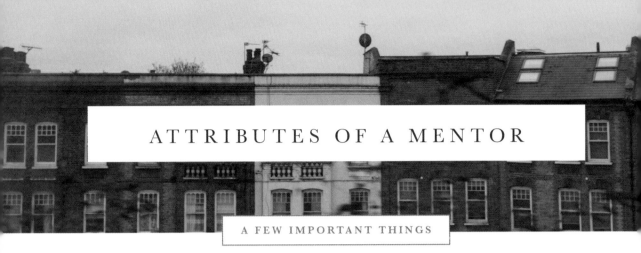

ATTRIBUTES OF A MENTOR

▶ A personal walk with Jesus is foundational!

▶ You'll need God to give you wisdom and discernment as you mentor.

▶ Be open and transparent about your life experiences.

▶ Be available for coffee—and for godly advice.

▶ Demonstrate godly character in all things.

▶ Share wisdom gained through your personal life experiences.

▶ Persevere. There'll be times when you feel like quitting, but know God has called you to this mentorship. You want to be faithful.

"Such is the confidence that we have through Christ toward God. Not that we are sufficient in ourselves to claim anything as coming from us, but our sufficiency is from God. … But we have this treasure in jars of clay, to show that the surpassing power belongs to God and not to us" (2 Cor. 3:4-5; 4:7, ESV).

This is not about us and our abilities. It's about making our lives and all that we've learned through the years available to those who are a season or more behind us, so they might benefit.

BEFORE YOU BEGIN

Setting appropriate expectations early in the process is key to a successful experience.

01. Learn what expectations your mentee has, if any. You may ask these three questions to help identify her expectations:
    ▶ Why do you desire to be in a mentoring relationship?
    ▶ What do you hope to gain from being mentored?
    ▶ What are your expectations of me as your mentor?

02. Take time to express your expectations for your mentee.
    ▶ Commitment: what she'll be asked to do.
    ▶ Time requirements: how often you will meet and for how long.

Content Will Guide the Conversation.

01. Focus on relevant topics, based on the mentee's needs.
02. Have a plan—prioritize the curriculum.
03. Meet regularly.

THINGS TO REMEMBER

    ▶ Rely on God.
    ▶ Have a big picture perspective.
    ▶ Celebrate her unique story.

EXPECTATIONS FOR MENTORS

- ▶ Mentor each woman in Jesus' name.
- ▶ Guide my mentee according to my experiences—share what I have learned.
- ▶ Consistently pray for my mentee.
- ▶ Love her, inspired by 1 Thessalonians 2:9 and 1 Corinthians 13.
- ▶ Believe in my mentee, and believe God for her.
- ▶ Live out what I am teaching.
- ▶ Be humble.
- ▶ Be transparent.
- ▶ Never give up on her.
- ▶ Be available.
- ▶ Maintain trust in the relationship.
- ▶ Hold her life and conversations with the highest confidentiality.
- ▶ Keep the end goal in focus.
- ▶ Make time and keep time set aside for my mentee.
- ▶ Create a safe space for my mentee to process, speak, and share.
- ▶ Respond with the love, grace, and truth of Jesus.
- ▶ Admit when I don't know the answers.
- ▶ Creatively find ways to encourage my mentee in her walk with Jesus and pursuit of Jesus.
- ▶ Sit under the authority of the Church's leadership team and trust their direction for the year. Forsake they in favor of we.
- ▶ Hold commitment over compatibility.
- ▶ Initiate, lead, and steward the relationship.
- ▶ Point my mentee to Jesus, not to myself.
- ▶ Be patient and walk at her pace, not my own.
- ▶ Hold the relationship with purpose and intentionality, without allowing it to become solely social.
- ▶ Have the courage to confront.
- ▶ Refuse to focus on my mentee's problems, remembering I am a guide, not someone who fixes.
- ▶ Pray she will apply wisdom and work out her own struggles with her eyes on Jesus.
- ▶ Display my own submission to Jesus.

There is great potential for meaningful and fruitful relationship between mentor and mentee. We believe these relationships can be rich soil for incredible growth. Reach out to your Church leadership and ask them to help encourage and protect your mentorship relationship. If a match is not experiencing a healthy connection beyond what is normal, consider consulting your Church leadership to help assess and consider whether or not you and your mentee(s) should continue meeting together. Work together to make a decision in the best interest of both mentor and mentee.

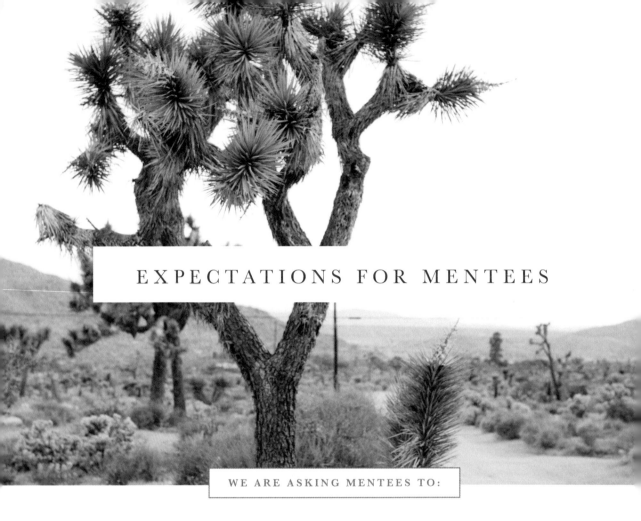

EXPECTATIONS FOR MENTEES

▶ Have focused time with Jesus five days a week.

▶ Complete assignments for each FLOURISH session throughout the year.

▶ Set goals and work diligently to reach them.

▶ Commit to predetermined meeting dates with mentor throughout the year, and make them a priority.

▶ Be punctual for meetings and respectful of their mentor's time.

▶ Be real and intentional in each meeting, making the most of the opportunity.

▶ Be accountable for assigned work. Be accountable in areas where it's been agreed that growth is needed.

MEETING GUIDELINES

A FEW TIPS FOR YOUR MEETINGS

We are beyond excited for all God has for you and your mentees in FLOURISH *this year! We are praying for you and believing that* FLOURISH's *best days are before us and trusting that God is already at work paving the way for you and your mentees.*

We've put together some thoughts and guidelines that you may find helpful in your monthly and group meetings.

Walk confidently in knowing that Jesus is your greatest champion, helper, guide, and resource for all you need as a mentor!

GROUP AND INDIVIDUAL MEETING OBJECTIVES

▶ INVEST: To meet regularly to build relationship and create consistent, ongoing opportunities to move into life with your mentees.

▶ SAFETY: To create a safe place for your mentees to process life, share their struggles, heartaches, concerns, joys, accomplishments, and prayer needs. Meeting with your mentees in your home is the best scenario for this.

▶ TRUE NORTH: To point them to Jesus and the Word, reminding them that He is all-sufficient, caring, confident, strong, bold, and poised to move on their behalf in every situation. Your goal as a mentor is to help them find answers in Scripture for their life questions.

▶ ACCOUNTABILITY: To be willing to ask hard questions, encourage them to keep their commitments, move into the mess, and bring accountability for worship, time in the Word, and prayer.

MEETING GUIDELINES
(continued)

▶ LISTEN: To listen well to their hearts and the deep dreams that are stirring in them. Cheer them on. Challenge them to live boldly for Jesus and to make Him their greatest pursuit.

▶ LOOK BACK TO LOOK FORWARD: To revisit goals you've set and/or previous prayer requests to see how they are doing in those areas.

▶ PRAY: To take seriously the powerful privilege of prayer and what it means to your mentees that you are someone who is truly invested in their lives and wants to go before the throne of God on their behalf.

The best way for you to be prepared to lead well in relationship with your mentees is to personally be committed to time with Jesus—in worship, the Word, and prayer. We're trusting that you're asking your mentees to go where you've already been walking!

We all know that if we're spending time in the same material our mentees are, we'll have so much more to offer and contribute to the conversation. So, even if the FLOURISH curriculum is not your main source of study, take time each week to learn what your mentees will be learning and spend some time in the books of the Bible they will be going through.

IN YOUR HOME:

During your meeting time, we strongly encourage you to invite your mentees into your home. This is a better environment for conversation and prayer—providing freedom and quiet to be able to truly "go there" together.

Keep a journal handy to write down specific things your mentees share for prayer. You may use this as a way to reconnect with them throughout the weeks beyond your meeting.

If it's entirely impossible to meet in your home, choose wisely when meeting in a public place. Look for a place where you'll be able to have privacy in conversation and room for prayer.

GROUP MEETING FORMAT

OBJECTIVES

▶ To bring all your girls together to allow for more connection and community.

▶ To create space for your girls to open up, share, talk life.

▶ To allow the girls to speak into one another's lives and encourage each other.

▶ To speak into their lives through the FLOURISH curriculum and through your own life experiences.

▶ To point them to Jesus and the Word.

EXAMPLE LAYOUT FOR A GROUP MEETING

Remember to text or email your girls a few days ahead to connect and let them know you're looking forward to being with them all.

▶ Allow 2 hours for your group meeting.

▶ Share dinner, dessert, snacks, drinks, etc., at the beginning of the night.

▶ Allow time for everyone to mingle and talk.

▶ Find a natural place in the conversation to transition to talking about what

▶ God has been revealing to them about Himself, focusing on the topic of the session (e.g. Whole and Holy, Beauty from Ashes, etc.). These topics may come from the FLOURISH curriculum, Sunday's message, a book they are reading, a Scripture they are memorizing, a conversation they had with someone, or other sources. Just invite them to share.

▶ Speak into the moment as the Holy Spirit leads.

▶ Allow space for mentees to speak into each other's lives.

▶ Encourage your girls to share goals and prayer requests so they can come around and encourage each other in those.

▶ Close out the night by praying over your girls, and if they are comfortable, allowing them to pray for each other.

Encourage your mentees to get involved by taking turns bringing a dessert or hosting in their homes if they're comfortable.

ONE-ON-ONE FORMAT

▶ Meet with your mentee individually as needed.

▶ Create the opportunity for her to share life.

▶ Listen and move into areas of life where she needs guidance and prayer.

▶ Point her to Jesus and the Word for answers.

EXAMPLE LAYOUT FOR A ONE-ON-ONE MEETING

▶ Text or email your mentee a day or two ahead of your meeting to let her know you're looking forward to time with her.

▶ Take time to talk and reconnect.

▶ Find out what's going on in life. Ask about her job, boyfriend, vacation, school, family, husband, kids, etc.

▶ Ask about her time with Jesus! How's that going?

▶ Discuss what God has been revealing to you both as you've spent time in the Word and prayer.

▶ Share Scripture and your own life experiences, as the Holy Spirit leads, to continue to further point her to Jesus.

▶ Write down specific prayer requests and take time to pray over her as you close out your time together.

SESSION ONE

THE FEMININE HEART

GOALS

- To help us see that we are designed by God for a unique and crucial purpose.

- To encourage us prioritize a relationship with God before concentrating on other relational roles.

- To understand and embrace our current season of life (single, wife, mother) as an opportunity to know God and serve Him more fully.

- To learn dependency on the Holy Spirit to enable us to thrive in our role as a single woman, wife and/or mother.

QUESTIONS

- How does understanding Eve help you understand yourself?

- What new discovery did you make about your role as a woman and how does that change the way you see yourself and interact with others?

- What's most challenging aspect of the season of life you are in right now?

- How can you know Jesus better through these challenges?

SESSION GOALS

WHOLE & HOLY

GOALS

- To embrace a new definition of what it means to be "healthy."

- To understand how spirit, soul and body are interdependent.

- To see how a relationship with Jesus can establish and/or alter our 'healthy living' goals

- To help us see service and worship of God as the new motivation for spiritual, emotional and physical health.

QUESTIONS

- Define what it means to be healthy? How should that definition be different for you as a believer?

- What are your healthy goals for your body? What about for your soul? Spirit?

- Which is most difficult for you? Why?

- Why is focusing on just physical fitness not enough to achieve true health? Is the same true when it comes to focusing only on emotional or spiritual health?

SESSION GOALS

UNDER NEW MANAGEMENT

GOALS

- To identify Jesus as Ruler of all and acknowledge His right to direct our lives

- To bring our lives in line with the teachings of Scripture in order to foster spiritual growth and development

- To loosen our dependence on possessions, habits, attitudes and/or relationships that block our devotion to Jesus.

- To help us see her ordinary tasks as usable by God for extraordinary purposes.

- To apply the mindset and mission of Jesus to all aspects of our lives.

QUESTIONS

- What's the difference between an owner and a manager? Apply that to your relationship to Jesus.

- Describe any changes that have been made in your life since you became under the new management of Jesus? What other changes need to be made?

- What area of your life (time, money, relationships, etc.) is the most difficult to turn over to Jesus? Why do you think this is the case?

- Sometimes it's hard to relate the events of Jesus' life to life right now. What challenge for living today do you take away from the Gospel of Mark?

SESSION GOALS

BEAUTY FROM ASHES

GOALS

- To help us see our disappointments and lost dreams in context of the sovereignty of God and as of use to Him for divine purposes.

- To affirm our conviction to do the right and godly thing even when it may cost us something.

- To guide us to embrace our opportunities and see ourselves as positioned in our current situation "for such a time as this." (Esther 4:14)

- To help us develop the skill of waiting on the Lord for His timing.

QUESTIONS

- God doesn't always reveal Himself in obvious ways. How have you seen Him move in the background of your life?

- What beautiful things in your life have grown out of the ashes of disappointment or heartache?

- What have you learned that can help you face future disappointments with confidence in God?

- Sometimes we play the role of Esther. Sometimes we are called to be like Mordecai. To whom can you be an encourager?

- How can you be the voice of faith in even impossible situations?

SESSION GOALS

SESSION FIVE

BE WELCOMED IN THIS PLACE

GOALS

- To help us recognize hospitality as a character trait of God.

- To guide us in seeing that true hospitality grows out of a relationship with Jesus.

- To widen the understanding of hospitality, taking it beyond the modern view of simply 'entertaining.'

- To lead us in developing a heart of hospitality that reaches beyond our family and friends.

- To remove common obstacles to opening our lives to others, and to encourage us to offer generosity to others right now.

QUESTIONS

- Often we want to welcome only friends and family. How do you see a different pattern emerging in God's actions toward you?

- What holds you back from or motivates you toward being hospitable and gracious toward others?

- How can you realign your thinking to extend hospitality to others but maintaining an attitude of service and worship of God?

- How can you practically 'love' those who you disagree with or who are difficult to be around?

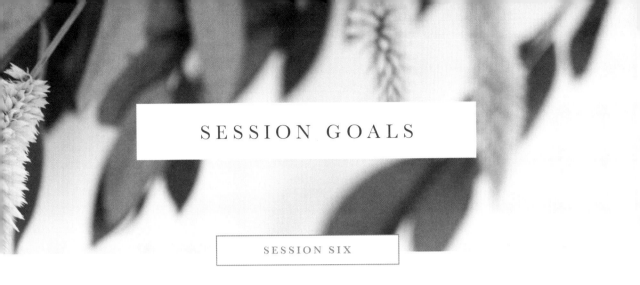

SESSION GOALS

STRONG & COURAGEOUS

GOALS

- To put our past mistakes behind and embrace a new future in the freedom God has provided through Jesus.

- To help us see all the experiences of our lives as preparation for God's call to serve Him.

- To guide us in developing a life-long pursuit of God.

- To learn to listen to and rely on the Holy Spirit as we face new (and seemingly impossible) tasks in the future.

- To trace God's caretaking hand in our past as an encouraging reminder of His presence and provision in our future.

QUESTIONS

- The world often encourages women to be 'strong and courageous'. How is the message of the world different from God's call toward strength and courage?

- In what area of your life do you find it most difficult to rely on God? Why?

- Recall a time when you lacked strength and courage. How did you get through it?

- What would you do differently now than you did then?

- What can you do now to prepare for the next big obstacle?

ABOUT THE TEAM

The FLOURISH team at Passion City Church is passionate about pointing women to Jesus through the power of His Word. A labor of love, this ministry has been shepherded by Daniele Flickinger, Susan Marks, and Shelley Giglio.

THE GROVE

The Grove is a monthly gathering of worship, teaching, and prayer for the women of Atlanta, Georgia. Hosted by Shelley Giglio and The Grove Team, these gatherings are an extension of what Jesus is doing in and through Passion City Church.

We believe every woman (person!) is God-designed, purpose-intended, significant, and lavishly loved by the King of the universe. No matter your age, your status, your style, or whether you think you have it all together or not, you are welcome at The Grove. If you live in Atlanta or are visiting the area, you are invited to come, rest, worship, learn, and be as we celebrate the power and greatness of Jesus. You can also follow along on The Grove Podcast. The heartbeat of The Grove is to encourage women to be rooted in the unfailing Word of God, to learn to flourish where we're planted, to walk in freedom in Christ and truly live, and to give our lives as shade to the people in our paths. This is The Grove.

PASSION CITY CHURCH

Rooted in the confession of Isaiah 26:8, Passion exists to glorify God by uniting students in worship, prayer, and justice for spiritual awakening in this generation. From its start in 1995, the Passion movement has had a singular mission—calling students from campuses across the nation and around the world to live for what matters most. For us, what matters most is the name and renown of Jesus. We believe in this generation and are watching God use them to change the climate of faith around the globe. Born out of the Passion Movement, Passion City Church exists to glorify God, to proclaim the name of Jesus to people in the city and the world. Passion City Church is located in Atlanta, Georgia, and Washington, DC, and is led by Senior Pastor Louie Giglio and his wife, Shelley.

THE GROVE
PODCAST

Hosted by Shelley Giglio and other women of The Grove, The Grove Podcast is designed to encourage women to become rooted in the Word of God, to flourish where they are planted, to walk in freedom with Jesus, and to offer their lives as shade to the people in their path.

subscribe and listen on iTunes and Spotify

THANK YOU

FLOURISH TEAM, PASSION CITY CHURCH

GENERAL EDITOR
Shelley Giglio

WRITERS
Susan Marks
Karen Woodall

EDITORS
Daniele Flickinger
Emily Vogeltanz
Aynsley Younker

CONTRIBUTORS
Theresa Anderson
Ashlee Campbell
Cara Dyba
Susan Marks
Regina Williams

ART DIRECTION
Meghan Brim
Ashlee Campbell

GRAPHIC DESIGNERS
Meghan Brim
Chandler Saunders
Kendra Harrell

PHOTOGRAPHY
Morgan Blake Photography

© 2019, 2020 Passion City Church, The Grove

All rights reserved. No portions of this book may be reproduced, stored in a retrieval system, or transmitted in any form or by any means---electronic, mechanical, photocopy, recording, scanning, or other---except for brief quotations in critical reviews or articles, without the prior written permission of the publisher.

Published in Atlanta, Georgia by Passion Publishing. Passion Publishing is an imprint of Passion, Inc.

passionpublishing

All Scripture quotations, unless otherwise indicated, are taken from the Holy Bible, New International Version®, NIV®. Copyright ©1973, 1978, 1984, 2011 by Biblica, Inc.TM Used by permission of Zondervan. All rights reserved worldwide. www.zondervan.com. The "NIV" and "New International Version" are trademarks registered in the United States Patent and Trademark Office by Biblica, Inc.TM Scripture quotations marked (ESV) are from the ESV® Bible (The Holy Bible, English Standard Version®). Copyright © 2001 by Crossway, a publishing ministry of Good News Publishers. Used by permission. All rights reserved. Scripture quotations from THE MESSAGE. Copyright © by Eugene H. Peterson 1993, 1994, 1995, 1996, 2000, 2001, 2002. Used by permission of NavPress. All rights reserved. Represented by Tyndale House Publishers, Inc. Scripture quotations taken from the New American Standard Bible® (NASB), Copyright © 1960, 1962, 1963, 1968, 1971, 1972, 1973, 1975, 1977, 1995 by The Lockman Foundation. Used by permission. www.lockman.org. Scripture quotations marked (AMP) are taken from the Amplified Bible, Copyright © 1954, 1958, 1962, 1964, 1965, 1987 by The Lockman Foundation. Used by permission.

Passion Publishing titles may be purchased in bulk for educational or business purposes. For information please contact admin@passionresources.com

ISBN: 978-1-949255-16-4 (wire-bound)

Printed in China

1 2 3 4 5 6 7 8 9 10